FREEDOM TO CHANGE

Four Strategies to Put Your Inner Drive into Overdrive

Michael Fullan

A Wiley Brand

ONTARIO
PRINCIPALS'
COUNCIL
Exemplary Leadership in Public Education

Cover Design: Wiley
Cover Image: ©iStock.com/enviromantic

Published by Jossey-Bass
A Wiley Brand
One Montgomery Street, Suite 1000, San Francisco, CA 94104-4594—www.josseybass.com

Jossey-Bass books and products are available through most bookstores. To contact Jossey-Bass directly call our Customer Care Department within the U.S. at 800-956-7739, outside the U.S. at 317-572-3986, or fax 317-572-4002.

Wiley publishes in a variety of print and electronic formats and by print-on-demand. Some material included with standard print versions of this book may not be included in e-books or in print-on-demand. If this book refers to media such as a CD or DVD that is not included in the version you purchased, you may download this material at http://booksupport.wiley.com. For more information about Wiley products, visit www.wiley.com.

Library of Congress Cataloging-in-Publication Data

Library of Congress Cataloging-in-Publication Data has been applied for and is on file with the Library of Congress.

ISBN 978-1-119-02436-1 (paper);
ISBN 978-1-119-02437-8 (ebk.);
ISBN 978-1-119-02438-5 (ebk.)

Printed in the United States of America

FIRST EDITION
HB Printing   10 9 8 7 6 5 4 3 2 1

ALSO BY MICHAEL FULLAN

Leading in a Culture of Change

The Principal: Three Keys to Maximizing Impact

The Six Secrets of Change: What the Best Leaders Do to Help Their Organizations Survive and Thrive

Change Leader: Learning to Do What Matters Most

Turnaround Leadership

Turnaround Leadership for Higher Education (with Geoff Scott)

Leading in a Culture of Change Personal Action Guide and Workbook

CONTENTS

To the "Freedom to" Heroes in the Field

ABOUT THE AUTHOR

MICHAEL FULLAN, ORDER OF CANADA, is professor emeritus at the Ontario Institute for Studies in Education, University of Toronto. He served as special adviser in education to Ontario premier Dalton McGuinty from 2003 to 2013, and now serves as one of four advisers to Premier Kathleen Wynne. He has been awarded honorary doctorates from the University of Edinburgh, University of Leicester, Nipissing University, Duquesne University, and the Hong Kong Institute of Education. He consults with governments and school systems in several countries.

Fullan has won numerous awards for his more than thirty books, including the 2015 Grawemeyer prize with Andy Hargreaves for *Professional Capital*. His books with Jossey-Bass include the best sellers *Leading in a Culture of Change, The Six Secrets of Change, Change Leader*, and *The Principal: Three Keys to Maximizing Impact*. To learn more, visit his website at www.michaelfullan.ca.

ONTARIO PRINCIPALS' COUNCIL

Exemplary Leadership in Public Education

Ontario Principals' Council

Exemplary Leadership in Public Education

Mission

To promote and develop exemplary leadership for student success in Ontario's schools

Purpose

The purpose of the Ontario Principals' Council is to:

- represent its membership
- promote the professional interests of its members
- support and protect its members
- advocate on behalf of public education
- provide professional growth opportunities for principals and vice-principals

Logo

There are three major components to the Ontario Principals' Council: the provincial structure, local OPC groups, and individual members. The logo represents the intersection of these components where all parts of OPC work together in support of the organization.

ACKNOWLEDGMENTS

Most of all I thank the great practitioners who give me insights all the time about leading educational change on a daily basis: Liz Anderson, Denise Belchetz, James Bond, Fred Brill, Davis Campbell, Lawrence DeMaeyer, Sophie Fanelli, Mary Jean Gallagher, Avis Glaze, Mike Hanson, Bill Hogarth, Lila Jenkins, Lyle Kirtman, Gabriela Mafi, John Malloy, Steve Martinez, Hazel Mason, Ian McFarlane, Andreas Meyer, Rick Miller, Scott Moreash, J Parappally, Christy Pichel, Michelle Pinchot, Tony Pontes, Jonathan Raymond, Joanne Robinson, Janet Schulze, Laura Schwalm, Sandy Thorstenson, Anita Simpson, Chris Steinhauser, Patrick Sweeney, Sue Walsh, Greg Whitby, and George Zegarac. A deep tribute to the late Greg Butler for his vision, friendship, and inspiration. To Joanne McEachen, Dolores Puxbaumer, Catie Schuster, and the gang at NPDL from around the world. Thanks also to the ever-stimulating Sir Michael Barber, and to Katelyn Donnelly. My great appreciation to Claudia Cuttress for coordinating production of the book and our various projects, and to the rest of my core team: Eleanor Adam, Joanne Quinn, Santiago Rincón-Gallardo, Terry Jakobsmeier, and Nancy Watson.

To Andy Hargreaves for his fresh ideas on matters of change. My gratitude to the great developmental editor Alan Venable, acquisitions editor Margie McAneny, production editor Mark Karmendy, and copy editor Michele Jones, who make Jossey-Bass such a fabulous publisher, and to Taryn Hauritz for the infographics.

Finally, to my immediate family, Wendy, Bailey, and Conor, who know how to balance and blend "freedom from" and "freedom to."

PREFACE

THIS BOOK EXAMINES THE CONCEPT of freedom for individuals and groups in the workplace. In the chapters that follow, I discuss the dynamics between freedom from constraints that stand in people's way of being happier and more productive, and freedom to pursue more satisfying alternatives. Although most of the discussion centers around freedom in the workplace, these ideas are equally applicable to your personal life.

The basic prescription is to put aside excuses that someone overhead is controlling things, and to tackle challenges directly oneself and with others. In this way, you will control more of your own success and have a chance of changing the system itself for the better. But as you gain more freedom from directives, "freedom to" is getting rid of constraints; "freedom from" is figuring out what to do when you become more liberated.

In the book I show that gaining greater freedom brings its own anxieties as well as opportunities. I spell out four guideposts for handling, indeed thriving, in this more complex "freedom to" world. It is a world where you will have to become both autonomous and cooperative, and you will need to deliberately seek feedback, learn to become more accountable, and interact more widely, which I call diffusion.

Another feature of this book and our work more generally is the notion of simplexity (coined by Jeff Kluger, 2008). For complex issues, we identify the smallest number of key factors (usually four to six), which is the simple part; then we try to make them gel, which is the complex part (given passions, politics, and personalities).

We are trying an innovation in this book, which is to produce a summary of each chapter in the form of visual infographics. We hope you find this practice interesting and useful. (Thanks to Taryn Hauritz for the infographics.)

The ideas in the book are intended to improve the lives of individuals as well as the organizations in which they work. Individual and system change is a two-way street. As you read this book, I suggest that you use it in two ways. First, apply the ideas to yourself—asking how you can rethink your own approach to change and development. Second, apply them in your relationships with others, both personally and at work. Be a leader for yourself and a leader with others.

⸰   ⸰   ⸰

To download the infographics and discussion questions found later in this book for workshops or your personal use, visit www.wiley.com/go/freedomchange.

FREEDOM
TO CHANGE

And yet precisely as that splendid historical moment dawned, a peculiar thing happened to me: When I arrived at work for the first time after my election, I found I was depressed. I was in some sort of profoundly subdued state. I felt strangely paralyzed, empty inside. I suddenly seemed to have lost all my ideas and goals, my skills, hope, and resolve. I felt deflated, spent, lacking in imagination. Even though just a few days earlier I had been terribly busy, I suddenly had no idea what I was supposed to be doing.

Vaclav Havel, the Salzburg Festival, July 26, 1990, on being elected president of Czechoslovakia after the "Velvet" Revolution.

CHAPTER · ONE

Freedom *From* or Freedom *To*

Most humans' lives are no longer "solitary, poor, nasty, brutish and short," as Thomas Hobbes had it in *Leviathan* in 1651. But surprisingly, given centuries of escalating innovations, we are not doing all that well when it comes to personal fulfillment. Moreover, things are not improving. Studies of the workplace find time and again that only a minority of people are satisfied with their working lives. The most recent Gallup (2014) survey of 350,000 employees found that only 30 percent of them saw themselves as engaged in the workplace. In a parallel study of 200,000 employees from more than five hundred organizations, 64 percent did not feel that they had a strong work culture, and 66 percent said that the opportunity for growth on the job was limited (TINYpulse, 2014). Ron Friedman (2014) finds similar low engagement of employees in the vast majority of organizations; he also reports that "the best companies to work for" (the minority) outperform the market by a factor of two to one (p. xiii). The percentage of disengaged workers has not changed for decades. This situation to me is a "freedom from" problem. There are factors keeping things the way they are, to no one's benefit, and nobody seems to be doing anything about it.

In my own field of education, as you go up the grade levels, higher percentages of students say that they are bored; teacher satisfaction has declined dramatically from 62 percent in 2008 to 38 percent in the present; and among principals, 75 percent say that their job has become too complicated. The trend is similar for school principals; since 2008, satisfaction has dropped from 68 percent to 59 percent (Metropolitan Life Insurance, 2013).

How do we change dreary daily working lives? "Freedom from" concerns what you can do to get rid of obstacles or other constraints.

What Do We Really Want?

The key question is, What will make people more fulfilled? There is growing evidence that there are a small number of factors at the heart of what motivates people to become engaged in worthwhile endeavors. Let's start with best-selling author Daniel Pink's book *Drive*. The research that Pink amasses is quite clear. For routine or rudimentary tasks that are more mechanical, extrinsic rewards such as money and punishment can motivate people to put in the effort to get results, but for any task that requires making independent decisions or problem solving, extrinsic rewards actually demotivate people. According to Pink's research, what is motivating are three factors: *a degree of self-directed autonomy, a sense of purpose,* and *mastery.* In my own work, I have added a fourth factor: *collaboration with peers to do something of value.* These are the intrinsic motivators: a feeling that you have a degree of autonomy in what you do and how you do it; a sense of purpose, that you are helping make your part of the world a better place; a growing mastery or expertise, meaning that you are becoming increasingly capable in your line of work; and a strong identity with colleagues, which gives you the sense that you are making a difference together.

Employees note these "drivers" when they are asked about what motivates their working lives. In the TINYpulse survey cited earlier, workers were asked to select among twelve factors the most important motivators for themselves. The top five in their estimation were camaraderie/peer motivation, intrinsic desire to do a good job, feeling encouraged and recognized, having a real impact, and growing professionally. Money was number seven. As Pink argues, you do have to pay people enough money to get the topic off the table. For "freedom to" people, money is a by-product of good work. It is not that money doesn't matter but rather that it is not the main driver. When the work itself is not satisfying, that is when money looms large as a factor. Money works in strange ways. The more that money is deployed as the main motivator, the more that intrinsic factors fall off the table, the less productive people become, and the less money is made. When the intrinsic factors are in play, people are more engaged and more productive, and more money is made.

The subject of this book is how to put intrinsic motivation factors into play for yourself and with others.

Motivational Drivers

- Some degree of self-directed autonomy

- Sense of purpose

- Mastery

- The rewards of collaborating with peers to do something of value

In a fundamental way, individual fulfillment and the evolution of humanity are intertwined. People are at their best when they are making a contribution in their own corner of the patch, leading both to personal satisfaction and to improvement in the world around them. We see from the surveys that most of us do not experience these motivators. But we could.

The starting point is to realize that the ball is in your court. The pursuit of fulfillment begins with you. It needs to be your own agenda. This book will guide you on this journey. To be successful, you will need to understand and engage in the dynamics of moving from "freedom from" to "freedom to."

If you had a magic wand that would remove all obstacles to change that you face, would you be better off? It may surprise you, but the evidence—both surface and deep—points in the opposite direction: you would find yourself facing new and more difficult challenges! The short answer to why this is so is that human beings are uncomfortable with pure freedom, and we unknowingly adapt by gravitating to worse alternatives. So the first matter—the subject of the rest of this chapter—is to get to the bottom of the paradox of freedom.

As you will see, in this book I have deliberately set out to advise individuals and the organization as a whole. Rather than focus on "leaders" in the most formal sense (something I have written about in my five previous books for Jossey-Bass), I have expanded the notion of leaders to include anyone who can and should take initiative. If these people happen to be formal leaders in an organization, all the better, because they can affect the lives of many. But I want to look at how *any* of us as individuals can work toward being free to change, while creating conditions that enable us to take advantage of this greater sense of freedom.

I start from the premise that being a leader and being a member of an organization have something in common or, perhaps more accurately, that both types should recognize that they have areas of converging interest, albeit often in tension. Any organization or system will benefit from the ideas, insights, and energy of all its members. And any individual will gain from being in an organization that is designed to draw on all its members in a social change process relative to a goal for the greater good. Seeking individuality—the fulfillment of humankind—in a social context is incredibly complex. The end game is not to be free and alone, but to be free with others. What makes humankind wonderful is the prospect of continuous realization of self, and human evolution through and with others.

A Double-Barreled Freedom

I was first stimulated to tackle these matters when I came across *The Freedom Report* from LRN (2014), a business management consultancy that "helps people and companies navigate complex legal and regulatory environments, foster ethical winning cultures, and inspire principled performance" (p. 19). This report of a study contains a framework that distinguished between "freedom from" and "freedom to" factors. The phrases reminded me of Eric Fromm's *Escape from Freedom* (1969) from my graduate school days as a sociologist in the making, so I went back and reread Fromm's book closely. Doing so opened a whole new line of thinking that was implicit in my current work, but had not been drawn out. (I will be discussing Fromm's work further in this chapter.)

LRN's main premise is that "when relationships are overly regulated and constrained, employees under-contribute, customers seek alternatives, and partnerships crumble" (2014, p. 3). The LRN study was based on a small sample (834 executives and professionals from large U.S.-based companies). LRN used a "freedom from/freedom to" framework to generate a Freedom Index, whereby executives rated the degree of constraint or freedom relative to four groups in their organizations: employees, customers, supply chain partners, and community groups. These executives were asked to rate what they thought their employees found constraining (in other words, those elements having to do with the "freedom from" problem). This list included hierarchical decision making, needless approvals, micromanagement, and the like. The main "freedom to" factors the executives identified included a culture based on shared values, and whether employees had the autonomy to structure their work and were encouraged to try new ideas. The organizations that scored higher on the index (meaning both greater "freedom from" and more "freedom to") performed much better on three key outcomes: financial performance (ten times higher than low-freedom companies), innovation, and long-term success.

But the LRN study did not go further into what exactly was going on in these successful organizations, how they had gotten to where they were, how applicable the ideas were to a range of situations, and especially how individuals—leaders or otherwise—could understand and learn to establish "freedom to" environments. This book is my attempt to go further with LRN's double-barreled "freedom from/freedom to" approach, to get inside these intriguing dynamics. Because my colleagues and I work in the fields of education and educational leadership—highly constrained systems, laden with fundamental "freedom from" limits—I pursue the issues mainly in that context, with forays into other fields, such as business, that have much in common with my own.

The Emptiness of "Freedom From"

Even if you are not of my generation, you may recognize the refrain of Kris Kristofferson and Fred Foster's song "Me and Bobby McGee," made famous by Janis Joplin:

> Freedom's just another word for nothing left to lose,
> And nothing don't mean nothing honey if it ain't free

It may be no accident that the lyrics in this song suited Janis Joplin and her brief life so well. "Freedom from," if we are not careful, can plunge us into despair and questions about the meaning of life. As Kristofferson seemed to know, "freedom from" may be happily intoxicating, but it's also a trap.

It may surprise you that the idea that freedom can turn out to be empty has a long psychoanalytic history, expressed most conspicuously in Eric Fromm's book. Fromm was a social psychologist, psychoanalyst, and sociologist who was born in 1900 in Germany to Orthodox Jewish parents and emigrated in 1933 as Nazism took over there. Meditating on these events, he saw that seeking individual freedom was a natural but false goal that inevitably got hijacked (and even hijacked itself) for worse alternatives. He sought to unravel this phenomenon, and concluded that freedom from constraints, what he called negative freedom, led to new deep problems. According to *Escape from Freedom,*

> Modern man, freed from the bonds of pre-individualistic society [medieval times], which simultaneously gave him security and limited him, has not gained freedom in the positive sense of realization of his individual self . . . Freedom, though it has

brought him independence and rationality, has made him isolated, and thereby anxious and powerless. This isolation is unbearable and the alternatives he is confronted with are either to escape from the burden of freedom into new dependencies and submission, or to advance to the full realization of positive freedom which is based on the uniqueness and individuality of man. (Fromm, 1969, p. x)

It turns out that "freedom from" is a hell of a lot easier to achieve than "freedom to." The evidence is that it is easier (and worse) to slip into new dependencies than it is to discover new individuality. Freedom from everything is to be isolated and anxious. Initially then, escaping from imposition is "to be alone and free, yet powerless and afraid" (Fromm, 1969, p. 34). In other words, attaining freedom is a subtle challenge, and our human vulnerabilities make us likely to mishandle the opportunity.

We do need to be free from constraints that channel us into dependency or lives of thoughtless repetition. But by itself, "freedom from" gives one "an increased feeling of strength, and at the same an increased isolation, doubt, skepticism—and resulting from all these—anxiety" (Fromm, 1969, p. 48). This natural anxiety can serve productive or destructive ends. The destructive or less-than-fulfilling alternatives are more common—a kind of human inertia. To be free in the negative sense is to be alone with oneself, "confronting an alienated, hostile world" (p. 150). Or, more conclusively, "Negative freedom by itself makes the individual an isolated being, whose relationship to the world is distant and distrustful and whose self is weak and constantly threatened" (p. 259).

Fromm states that the anxiety of negative freedom is fundamentally intolerable and results in at least three negative outcomes, which he discusses at some length: authoritarianism, destructiveness or self-destruction, and conformity.

Fromm wanted to understand authoritarianism as a mechanism that contributed to the rise of Nazism in Germany. In his view, succumbing to authority resolves the psychological problem of negative freedom. Likewise, in daily life we submit to lesser forms of authoritarianism—for example, when we stay in destructive relationships. Destructiveness or self-destruction refers to personal breakdowns, suicide being the ultimate example. The anxieties of freedom that Fromm describes help explain why even people who seem to have it all engage in self-destructive actions. In short, gaining greater freedom is fraught with new difficulties.

Much of what we want to do requires us to operate within the contexts of hierarchical organizations. Ironically, the more the performance of the organization comes into question, the more that leaders lay on additional requirements. The field of education is a prime example. Higher authorities, perverse mandatory testing, bad leadership, unions, sheer workload, bureaucracy, annoying peers—the list goes on—all of these limit what we (think) we can do and grind many of us to a halt.

This need not be. The first positive step we can take is to realize that we may not be as stuck as we think. My favorite example (and I got it from the horse's mouth) comes from a superintendent of education whom I know very well. Let's call her "Rebel with a Cause." She and her senior team in the district found that they were constantly called on to respond to mindless compliance requirements from the state department of education, filing report after report that they were pretty sure no one read.

One June in the press of year-end chores, they received a major request from the state that required compiling reams of data. The staff was under huge duress as they contemplated how to meet the target. Hating to see needless anxiety, this is what Rebel did: She asked two staff members to write the beginning and end sections of the report—a few pages—and said she would take care of the rest. Then, between the two sections, she inserted a copy of Tolstoy's *War and Peace* (one of the longest novels ever written).

The staff begged Rebel not to submit the document ("We'll get in trouble," "You'll get fired," and so on). She reassured them that it was highly unlikely that there would be repercussions and said that if the latter happened, she would buy the team a dinner. They then submitted the report electronically (which caused the system to shut down temporarily—a frequent occurrence). She never heard back from the state department, and bought her staff dinner anyway!

As I discussed this incident with her she said,

> The reason I did this was not to annoy the state or to shut down their system. I did it only to try to make a point with some of my staff who worried themselves sick and spent far too many hours to comply with the endless and often repetitive requests from multiple siloed departments in the state department.

However, please don't begin to think that arbitrary defiance is the answer to your own bureaucratic harassments. We will return to Rebel later; but let me just mention here that, as we shall see, the reason she was so confident was that she had a strong set of "freedom to" guideposts; she had a strong moral compass and knew what she wanted to accomplish with powers of flexibility.

Another example from education of the limits of "freedom from" comes from my work in understanding "school autonomy." Several jurisdictions have responded to the constant complaints from school principals that they have limited freedom to act given all the bureaucratic requirements laid on by the hierarchy. In Australia, for example, some states have passed new policies whereby individual schools can apply for "independent public schools" status, which gives them more freedom. There has not yet been systematic documentation of the consequences, but some of the various educators with whom I have discussed this change refer to "learned helplessness"; that is, people are so used to being directed that they find it difficult to take advantage of the new flexibility. In other cases, schools go off on their own, failing to remain "connected" to the system. (I will discuss what I call "connected autonomy" in chapter 3, "Autonomy and Cooperation.")

As I prepared for this book, I asked some leading educators I know (teachers, principals, superintendents, and others) to draw on their experiences to respond to certain questions. From time to time I will quote members this group, whom I refer to as "the select dozen." One question I asked was whether they had ever experienced obtaining new freedoms only to find new concerns. Most had. For example:

> I recall being freed from a demanding and at times vindictive immediate supervisor who got transferred. The ensuing year was filled with initial relief. At the same time, the freedom

created uncertainty for me and doubt about whether I was doing "the right things."

—*Secondary school principal*

The school district had always controlled the technology put into our schools with great authority. As students' use of technology grew in demand, teachers' use increased, and as the world became more connected through the Internet and person-to-person networks, I wanted the constraints that the school board placed on Internet access, technology purchase, and allowing technology to be reduced, so that we could make those decisions at the school level. I thought student learning and teaching would take off, and everyone would be on board with these changes. Initially, students, teachers, and parents were all scared of the change. We had to move from an anxious and isolated place to a place where people came together to make new practices work.

—*Elementary principal*

Two respondents gave more personal examples:

When my mother passed away, I thought I would feel a sense of freedom because I had been so absorbed in her care. I expected to devote all of the free time to doing things for myself. Instead I felt at loose ends and unsettled.

—*District supervisor*

I was adopted. When I finally found my birth mother, I was free from the wondering that had regularly occupied me in the past, wondering about where and whom I had come from. Who was I? It was a constant wonder in my life. At age thirty-one, I did get to meet my birth mother. I finally had a few of the answers to many questions I'd had over the course of my life, but rather than feel comfort or liberation, I instead felt deflated and disappointed. I realized that my story could no longer be left entirely to my imagination. Instead of being "anybody," I was somebody, and this little four-foot-nothing, bubbly, white-haired, chatty woman was my mother.

—*District supervisor*

All four respondents said that they had to figure out how to handle the new freedom. Stated another way, being rid of the burden of constraints is followed by new challenges.

Constraints Don't Need to Stop Us

Before crossing the bridge to "freedom to," let's develop a mind-set that constraints are not action stoppers. Ryan Holiday, a media strategist and prominent writer on strategy and business, lays the foundation in his book *The Obstacle Is the Way* (2014). He catalogues the constraints:

> Systemic: decaying institutions, rising unemployment, sky-rocketing costs of education, and technological disruption. Individuals: too short, too old, too scared, too poor, too stressed, no backers, no confidence . . . [And] the responses they elicit: Frustration. Confusion. Helplessness, Depression. Anger. (p. 1)

But obstacles, like mountains, are there to be crossed. Overcoming obstacles, says Holiday, begins with how we look at specific problems. Just like our superintendent Rebel, people on the move from "freedom from" see obstacles for what they are: things to be broken down, understood, and overcome. It is their attitude, philosophy, and ingenuity (ability and confidence) to solve a problem that makes the difference. People with this orientation tend to see obstacles as problems to be solved; and with practice they get better and better at dealing with what stands in their way, including handling difficulty and defeat.

Most of us do not even try Plan A, which should be refusal to be stymied by obstacles; rather, we tend to see them as more fixed than they are. Before proceeding, take stock of your current situation by addressing the following points:

- List the main obstacles standing in your way with respect to your personal and/or organizational goals.

- How could you minimize or overcome some of these obstacles by breaking them down and taking creative action?

As you get better at addressing constraints, you will then need Plan B, so to speak, when "freedom from" by itself is not enough because it does not consider the changes that liberation is likely to require for success. If Fromm is correct, newfound freedoms leave us consciously or subconsciously too alone in a hostile world. Subsequent chapters in this book are largely about the details of developing your own Plan B—what you will need to know to live productively in the "freedom to" world that you will help create.

A Direction for Freedom *to* Change

Fromm was mainly concerned with identifying the vulnerability of detached freedom, which in his analysis could lead to psychological breakdown or succumbing to authoritarian domination. He only hinted at the positive solution, which he discussed under the heading of "Character and the Social Process," relegated to an appendix of his book. Here are some hints:

> Man's inalienable rights of freedom and happiness are founded in inherent human qualities: his striving to live, to expand and express the potentialities that have developed in him in the process of historical evolution . . .

> The fundamental approach to human personality is the understanding of man's relation to the world, to others, to nature and to himself. We believe that man is *primarily* a social being. (1969, pp. 287–288, italics in the original)

Thus the fundamental problem and solution for Fromm was wrapped up in the psychology of interpersonal relationships. This is the point of departure for our perspective on "freedom to." The gist of the solution is to pursue meaningful goals and values through complex autonomous-connected relationships with others.

Take Action

Look back at your responses to the two bulleted suggestions listed earlier. As a further prelude to your pursuit of better outcomes, try spelling out what you would do with more freedom:

☐ Identify one or more goals—even small ones—that you would like to tackle in your workplace or personal life.

☐ How would you initially go about pursuing these goals?

Next

The rest of this book is a guide to maintaining and mining a "freedom to" existence. Chapter 2 will say more about simplexity—distinguishing it from strategy, for example. Chapters 3 through 6 will pursue the four core factors essential for reconciling the "freedom from/freedom to" conundrum:

- Autonomy *and* cooperation
- Feedback
- Accountability
- Diffusion (by interacting more widely)

These four themes are guideposts for maximizing "freedom to change." To be clear, you find your best freedom *through* continuously navigating your way within and among the four. In brief then, my theory of action addresses how you can come to understand and engage in this quartet of factors and their interactions.

The processes for mastering any one of the four—not to mention figuring out how to orchestrate them—are complex. I admit we are talking about difficult change processes. But be assured that my colleagues and I know a fair amount about the practical dos and don'ts of change. It is time to figure out how to put your inner drive into overdrive.

'FREEDOM FROM' OR 'FREEDOM TO'?

Understand the dynamics between 'freedom from' constraints that hinder happiness and productivity, and 'freedom to' pursue more satisfying alternatives.

'FREEDOM TO'
Not as easy as it seems!

What would you do if you faced fewer barriers?

'FREEDOM FROM'
How to change dreary daily working lives.

What can you do to get rid of obstacles or other constraints?

Only 30% of people see themselves as engaged in the workplace.
(Gallup survey of 350,000 employees, 2014)

Most people believe that if all their obstacles to change were removed, they'd be better off.

Surprisingly, evidence suggests that you would have new and more difficult challenges to face!

WHAT DO WE REALLY WANT?

>> some degree of self-directed autonomy

>> sense of purpose

>> sense of mastery

>> rewards of collaborating with peers to do something of value

THE DECEPTION OF FREEDOM

'freedom from' may be alluring but it's also a trap.

Freedom from everything is to be isolated and anxious.

'freedom from' by itself does not consider the changes that liberation requires for success.

We need to know what to do with these new freedoms.

Constraints are not action stoppers.

Obstacles, like mountains, are there to be surmounted.

Freedom is a subtle challenge. Our human vulnerabilities make us likely to mishandle the opportunity.

The first positive step we can take: Realize that we may not be as stuck as we think.

'Freedom to' goalposts

Autonomy and cooperation

Feedback

Accountability

Diffusion by interacting more widely.

The end game is not to be free and alone, but to be free with others.

CHAPTER · TWO

Simplexity as a Guide for Change

S implexity is about finding workable solutions to problems when situations appear too complex. The term was coined by Jeff Kluger, senior editor and writer for *Time*, and developed in a book in 2008. In it he gives many examples of "why simple things become complex" and "how complex things can be made simple."

My own spin on the term is compatible with his basic ideas, but geared toward taking action in situations that seem beyond our control and comprehension. For my purposes here, *simplexity* means taking a complex issue and, first, identifying the smallest number of key, alterable factors that would make a big difference. In our case, these are the four factors that form the subjects of chapters 3 through 6. This first part is relatively simple. The second, more challenging step is making these factors gel by interrelating them in given situations where politics, power, and the pressures of our lives enter in. Each one of the components is critical, but the interaction effect of the four working together is what generates the impact. Chapter 1 briefly noted the four factors that I believe are central to increasing one's freedom to change: autonomy and cooperation, feedback, accountability, and diffusion. Get these four factors right and you will have a strong "freedom to" action agenda, thereby productively filling the void created by "freedom from."

Recall Rebel's apparently defiant act in dealing with unreasonable requests from the state. This was definitely a "freedom from" stance. Yet the reason she was able to act so confidently is that she knew what to do with her "freedoms to." As she put it:

My "why" as a superintendent was very simple—to ensure that every child in our system received the same educational opportunities and success that I would have wanted for my own children. To that end, all decisions I made had to pass the "why test."

—*Superintendent Rebel*

In short, she had no trouble filling, indeed creating, the "freedom to" opportunities because she has an uplifting positive agenda. Her district, by the way, zoomed up the performance charts compared to other districts in the state.

At this point, you may not have as clear a compass as Rebel. You may be closer to the position Arianna Huffington was in when she received a severe but lucky wake-up call. Not to say she wasn't succeeding as cofounder of the Huffington Post Media Group, but her critical story begins on April 6, 2007, when she came to consciousness lying on the floor of her home office in a pool of blood. She had collapsed from exhaustion and hit her head on the corner of her desk, cutting her eye and breaking her cheekbone. She had spent the previous two years since the founding of *Huffington Post* at an incredible pace "working eighteen hours a day, seven days a week, trying to build our business, expand our coverage, and bring in investors" (Huffington, 2014, p. 1). On the surface, she was one of the most successful people in the media business. In our terms, she had pigged out on "freedom to," making her life worse, not better. Her book *Thrive: The Third Metric to Redefining Success and Creating a Life of Well-Being, Wisdom, and Wonder* tells her story subsequent to her collapse. Huffington set out to redefine her life, making lasting improvements focusing on what she called "the third metric."

The first two metrics Huffington had in mind were power and money, of which she had plenty. The third, missing metric was a set of what she calls four pillars: well-being, wisdom, wonder, and giving. Huffington refashioned her life to make the third metric a new pillar of her existence. Her new motto, and her advice to others, became, Don't just take your place in the world, but be part of changing it for the better. Note that Huffington retains power and money as important metrics, but they only make sense when accompanied by the third metric of well-being. The three in concert make a life.

We are beginning to get a sense of how deeply difficult it is to find the solution to Fromm's "escape from freedom." In the face of all kinds of obstacles, some of them subconscious within us, as they were for Huffington (and Rebel, I'm sure), we have to figure out our own place in life and, in fact, in humanity. Even if we are not household names or highly placed, we need to live a productive "micro-life" in a context of consequential macro stakes. As Huffington sees it, "Something as vast and epic as the destiny of humanity depends on something as intimate and personal as the shape of our individual lives" (p. 258). At the same time, the problem is that

> there are almost no worldly signals reminding us to stay connected to the essence of who we are, to take care of ourselves along the way, to reach out to others, to pause to wonder, and to connect to that place from which everything is possible. (p. 261)

Rebel and Huffington were lucky enough to have or discover some core values that guided their actions and developments. But what if your personal values are not so clear, or you simply feel stuck in your situation? My advice is to embrace simplexity: finding your way through action guided by a small number of factors. I say "small number" because anything else will be too complicated. As I said, the simplexity approach involves identifying what those factors are and how you might enact them in concert.

Perhaps the best way to expand on simplexity as a concept is by considering how it differs from strategic thinking, which might have a similar ring. Before I do so, however, I will call attention to a pair of words that can also be confusing: *complex* and *complicated*. I do not use these words interchangeably. When I say "complex," I mean a quality that is generally inherent in a problem. Chess, for example, is a highly complex game, in part because the player must combine the efforts of six different kinds of pieces (kings, queens, knights, and so forth) that must follow six very different sets of rules dictating how they advance on the board. There's no getting around the inherent complexity of chess. By contrast, "complicated" embraces other factors that may not be inherent in the nature of the game. For example, a player can complicate a game of chess by getting no sleep the night before or entering the game distracted by hunger or anger.

Every problem has some essential degree of complexity, and simplexity is a way of keeping it manageable as events unfold. A simplexity mind-set identifies a small number of potentially interrelated parts that can feed on each other. By contrast, complication often adds layers of disconnected pieces that end up making matters worse. Ironically, some ways of attempting to deal with complex problems, when carried too far, merely add complications of their own. Consider the long and honorable tradition of *strategy*—attempts to anticipate in advance how the details of events might unfold.

The Limits of Strategy

Let's stand back and consider what we know about change. It turns out that, in the name of strategy, we often have made change far more complicated than it need be. The problem is that as we strive for complexity in our strategic plans, we end up generating clutter. In this regard, it is fascinating to consider the history of the concept of strategy—originally the idea of maximizing what one can accomplish in difficult situations by planning one's actions according to conditions and contingencies. A good idea, except for the changing nature of reality.

Lawrence Freedman (2013) wrote the definitive book on strategy—all seven hundred–plus pages of it—tracing the concept from biblical times to the present. I draw from his account in the following paragraphs.

The concept of strategy derives in the first place from military thought. An early thinker about military strategy, Carl von Clausewitz, born in 1780, learned his craft in the Prussian army as it failed to resist Napoleon's. One of his conclusions foreshadows where our analysis is heading:

> Everything in war is simple, but the simplest thing is difficult. The difficulties accumulate and end by producing a kind of friction that is inconceivable unless one has experienced war . . . Countless minor incidents—the kind you never really foresee—combine to lower the general level of performance, so that one always falls short of the intended goal. (quoted in Freedman, 2013, p. 87)

Freedman captures the spirit of approaching unforeseeable situations when he quotes another of Napoleon's opponents, the aged Russian general Mikhail Kutuzov (remarkably portrayed in Tolstoy's *War and Peace*). Kutuzov's best advice before going into battle was to get a good night's sleep: "immediate attentiveness to unfolding possibilities was going to be more valuable than forward planning" (Freedman, 2013, p. 102).

This notion of paying more attention to the reality of action than to theoretical strategy is also depicted by one of von Clausewitz's followers, von Moltke, who declared in 1870 that "no plan survived contact with the enemy" (Freedman, 2013, p. 104). Or if you prefer a more contemporary philosopher, the boxer Mike Tyson observed: "Everyone has a plan til they get punched in the mouth" (p. ix).

The more complicated things become in highly detailed plans, the less likely that a rational solution can take everything into account, as Freedman so wonderfully concludes in this passage quoting Harry Yarger, a teacher at the US Army War College:

> So much was expected of the true strategist: a student of the present who must be aware of the past, sensitive to the possibilities of the future, conscious of the danger of bias, alert to ambiguity, alive to chaos, ready to think through the consequences of alternative courses of action, and then able to articulate all of this with sufficient precision for those who must execute its prescriptions. (p. 238)

It is unlikely that a single individual could be this good. Pure control, in short, is an illusion, and our attempts to completely control a situation make matters worse. To get a good night's sleep might have sounded at first like thin advice, but maybe it wasn't so bad. (Still, I believe we can do better and keep the sleep as well.)

Societies are increasingly complex, and we try to control the situation through strategies and plans that themselves become more and more complicated. Adding complication to the complex produces . . . well, you get the drift.

Control versus Clutter

As I suggested at the outset, simplexity involves identifying a small number of factors that can serve us in the heat of action and guide our thinking before and after.

To survive and possibly even thrive, we need simplexity thinking and action for ourselves because policymakers and planners can never solve our problems from above. It is not so much that we need to escape from policymakers (an impossibility) but rather that we need to figure out how to respond to policies with greater freedom of action relative to our own agenda. This is why in my educational work I advise teachers, principals, superintendents, and others that it is not their job to implement state policy literally but rather to "exploit" it, not as rebels but as local actors with transparent values and goals.

If we don't take independent action, we will be left with ever unworkable solutions, as those above us try to control the uncontrollable. For example, in an attempt to control implementation, rational strategists make matters worse by establishing processes that require people to do things that by and large will not, cannot work because they are inflexible to the realities of implementation. And as managers realize that the planning-implementation model does not work, their first reaction seems to be to add more rigidity to the model rather than to loosen it up. Yves Morieux and Peter Tollman (2014) clearly document this pattern. They show how requirements for companies—and I would say *any* organization—"have become more numerous, are changing faster, and what's more, are often in conflict with one another" (p. 5). Applying their own "Complexity Index" to a large sample of organizations, they found that business complexity/complication has multiplied sixfold since 1955.

Morieux and Tollman (2014) concluded that as layers of complication are added to complexity, progress becomes even more unlikely as performance and engagement come almost to a halt. As they observe, "Over the past fifteen years the number of procedures, vertical layers, interface structures, coordination bodies, scorecards, and decision approvals has increased dramatically—between 50 percent and 350 percent depending on the company" (p. 7).

A prime example of the folly of pursuing complexity and ending up with clutter comes from my own recent study of new developments in the school principalship (Fullan, 2014). Policymakers have taken the finding from research that the principal should be an instructional leader in the school, and overinterpreted it. In several states and scores of school districts, they have redefined the principal's job to include one-on-one teacher appraisal in order to give feedback to teachers for improvement. Along with this, a new layer of bureaucracy has been added at the district level: people whose responsibility it is to supervise principals; they are, in other words, responsible for supervising the supervisors. I call this micromanagement madness. There are not enough hours in the day to carry out this task, not to mention that it is fundamentally alienating for both teachers and principals.

A recent study by the Organization for Economic Cooperation and Development (2014b) in its Teaching and Learning International Survey (TALIS) project confirmed the inevitable outcome. Over 50 percent of teachers surveyed in thirty-four countries reported that their principals conducted teacher appraisal "simply to fulfill administrative requirements." In *The Principal*, I offered an alternative that has been well documented as successful in practice: that principals should act as "lead learners," participating with teachers in "using the group to change the group" (Fullan, 2014). Employing this approach, principals are highly effective in developing focused collaborative cultures with teachers. They thus affect learning outcomes for students indirectly, but nonetheless explicitly.

In company settings, without such a shift to enabling and mobilizing the group, you get what Morieux and Tollman (2014) found: managers spending up to 60 percent of their time in monitoring and coordinating meetings (which the authors call "work on work"). These same companies, predictably enough, have high proportions of disengaged employees. Morieux and Tollman's findings are corroborated by Khosla and Sawhney's study of successful organizations (2014). What works, they say, is to focus, cut complexity, strive for simplicity, and communicate with clarity and candor—qualities they find missing in most firms.

All of this is to say that bosses who make things ever more complicated are even worse than bosses who are just bossy. When the work is complex, rather than restrict options (layering on requirements that motivate people to seek "freedom from"), we do better by creating conditions and mechanisms that increase "freedom to" actions that are satisfying and productive for the individual and the organization. Most jobs today have unpredictable aspects. These jobs, certainly teaching, require discretionary problem solving. What worked on the assembly line cannot work under conditions that require independent judgment.

To revisit our discussion about complication versus complexity, the latter has a lot to do with interconnectedness. It concerns the whole and its interrelated parts. The way to manage a complex problem or situation is not to add yet more complicating requirements that attempt to anticipate every possible outcome but instead to figure out the small number of key forces at work, and leverage their interaction effects.

"Freedom From" Isn't Victory

I've just argued in favor of "freedom from" in the sense of reducing clutter and removing ineffective constraints or prescriptions. And a frame of mind of "freedom from" is useful in starting a process of change. With it, you begin to find choices. As Rebel demonstrated, you may be stuck with the policies laid on by bosses, but you are not stuck with their mind-sets. And for additional solace, you may become aware, as she did, that the more intricate and complicated the rules become, the harder it is for authorities to monitor them.

But let me reiterate a caution against prematurely declaring victory when you have managed simply to remove constraints. People make that leap only to find that "freedom from" is not the same as "freedom to." Two examples from education make the point.

Many of us have complained about the problem of over-testing students, especially if the results are tied to punitive accountability. To remove bad testing schemes is only half the problem, as the Welsh found out the hard way. Wales discontinued its state tests in 2004, breaking away from the system deployed in England. At that point it declared victory, only to discover that Welsh student results in literacy and numeracy have continued to decline over the past decade, so that in 2014, Welsh educators found themselves reintroducing national literacy tests. (Whether this will turn out to be a true "freedom to" victory will depend on what they know about the issues I raise in subsequent chapters of this book.) What the Welsh did was get rid of an unwanted constraint, but they then failed to work on an alternative better solution. In short, replacing a negative thing with nothing is not the answer.

Another "example"—hypothetical in the sense that it has not yet happened, but in my view predictably will—is that teachers' unions and others in the United States and elsewhere are lobbying fiercely against certain current forms of teacher evaluation that assess each and every teacher and link the results to teacher pay increases. All the evidence is that this system does not and cannot work on a large scale. Because it is a bad idea, it will fail, and the policies will be rescinded. But that will not be enough. The answer is not just to erase bad things but also to replace them with better things—in this case, feedback that leads to improvement. If you don't rely on teacher evaluation as the solution to improvement, what is a better alternative to maximize effective feedback? (See chapter 4.)

Constantly reducing the impact of constraints—addressing the "freedom from" problem—is the easier aspect of finding freedom, because one can concretely see the ineffectiveness of being overmanaged. A much harder problem, because the solution is more sophisticated and because it has not yet already been implemented on any scale, is the "freedom to" aspect. Becoming free from constraints may feel good at the beginning, but soon the next and more vexing challenge presents itself: Where in this newfound freedom do you find cohesion that is not equally confining?

The basic idea of simplexity actually preceded Kluger. It can be found in earlier work, especially the harbinger writings of Vilfredo Pareto, the Italian sociologist who in 1906 gave us the deceptively simple 80–20 rule that came to be known as Pareto's Principle (see Livingston, 1935). Pareto noticed in several complex areas that 80 percent of effects come from 20 percent of the causes. For example, if you were to try to identify and work on all possible causes of a given problem, you would get hopelessly bogged down, but if you were to select a small number of high-yield factors and work on them relentlessly, you would get further, and then could build on these early successes. The more complex the problem, the more you need simplexity as your approach. For example, in this book I have taken something as profound as the "freedom from/freedom to" axis and reduced it to four big interrelated factors.

Simplexity, with its small number of high-leverage factors, is a way to go about focusing on Pareto's notional 20 percent of factors, implementing them well in concert over time and reaping his notional 80 percent benefits.

More than one hundred years after Pareto, we live in a much more complicated world, and we know more about the variety of causes and effects. We know too much, so to speak, which makes it difficult to figure out where to start. With the idea of simplexity, we have a handle on how to think about and act on complex problems. Improving health is a good example. You can make it complicated by identifying a long list of factors and remedies, or make it overly simple by seeking a magic bullet in the form of vitamins and prescription pills. Or you can go the simplexity route: eating a better diet, exercising three times a week, and getting eight hours sleep every night.

But simplexity entails a second element, beyond Pareto: once having identified the smallest number of high-leverage factors relative to a problem you would like to solve, you face a further challenge of how to manage those factors. This will be the subject of chapters 3 through 6.

Take Action

In your own situation, reflect on the following:

☐ How have I made my own situation or pursuit of goals overly complicated?

☐ Am I already applying simplexity thinking in some corner of my work or private life? Can I generalize that to other areas?

☐ Have any of my peers or team recently expressed a frustration that they might address with simplexity thinking?

Take a specific goal or priority that is important to you and identify the smallest number of key factors (five or fewer, for example) that you could focus on that might make a significant difference in your progress on the priority.

Next

This brings us to the point of how to proceed on the "freedom to" agenda. In our terms, you have to understand how autonomy and cooperation can coexist, how feedback can be maximized for learning, how accountability can be present and effective, and how diffusion works to enable us to interact productively more widely. And you have to be aware of how these four factors feed on each other. Succeeding chapters develop each one. Get these four factors right in combination, and you will be well on your way to freedom and fulfillment. Let's begin the simplexity journey.

SIMPLEXITY

A guide for change . . .

Finding workable solutions to problems when situations appear too complex.

Take a complex issue and identify the smallest number of key, alterable factors that would make a big difference.

Make these factors gel in given situations where politics, power, and the pressures of our lives enter in.

A 'freedom from' frame of mind is useful in starting a process of change.

Freedom to change depends on understanding the dynamics of change within each factor, and their interactions.

AUTONOMY/ COOPERATION

FEEDBACK

ACCOUNTABILITY

DIFFUSION

Get these to gel right and you will productively fill the void with a solid 'freedom to' agenda.

Use 'freedom to' as a deliberate opportunity to make lasting improvements.

INTERACTION GENERATES IMPACT

TAKE INDEPENDENT ACTION!

"Something as vast and epic as the destiny of humankind depends on something as intimate and personal as the shape of our individual lives."
Huffington

Master the factors and their interactions and you are ready to be as free and as effective as a human can be.

CHAPTER · THREE

Autonomy and Cooperation

One of the four keys to having a good life at home and at work is to sort out the autonomy-cooperation conundrum. If you err on the side of being on your own, you lack the human connection essential for life. If you are in a bad relationship, you may be better off alone, but once alone, you are stuck with yourself. Prolonged isolation is unhealthy. Similarly, if you succumb to the extreme of being absorbed in the group, you lose your identity. It is not that you *plan* to be too alone or too involved; it just happens. "Freedom to" places you in this world of danger and opportunity. But this chapter tells you that you have choice there, and lays out some ideas for striking a healthy balance between being your own person and being connected.

In chapter 1, I referred to Dan Pink's three motivational drivers: a degree of self-directed autonomy, a sense of purpose, and mastery. In this chapter, I build on the nature and importance of autonomy, and also link it to a key motivational factor that Pink did not identify, namely "relatedness to others," which I call *cooperation.* Why cooperation and not collaboration or teamwork? Perhaps the best way to answer this is to borrow a good footnote from Morieux and Tollman (2014), whose work on complexity in companies I introduced in chapter 2:

> Cooperation is often used synonymously with coordination or collaboration . . . Collaboration is about teamwork as people get along, based on feelings and good interpersonal relationships . . . such relationships often lead to the avoidance of real cooperation in the interest of maintaining convivial relations within the group or team . . . Coordination refers to allocating an order of some sort among pre-defined activities that have to be made compatible. Scientific management can only

at best obtain coordination by means of procedures, interface structures, metrics and incentives. Cooperation, by contrast, involves directly taking into account the needs of others in creating a joint output . . . [T]here is a clear emphasis on joint goal, output, and result. Cooperation contains a notion of shared intentionality; we define objectives together and share the outcome. (2014, pp. 198–199)

My focus, however, is not on what cooperation might connote in terms of a group's output, but on its spirit of connection. Recall that Fromm argued that as we gain greater freedom from constraints, we are vulnerable to isolation, aloneness, and dysfunctional anxiety. In other words, being alone is an "inhuman condition," if you will. Only some form of "belonging" with others in the service of worthwhile goals makes us fully human. Being our own person and being connected is the core tension and challenge of living meaningfully.

Connectedness in Action

The deeper meaning of connectedness is not always easy to identify, but the next two sections may be helpful. The first looks mainly at an individual's perspective, the second more at groups.

One Member of a Crew

This example comes from the true story, told by Daniel Brown (2014) in *Boys in the Boat,* of how nine boys from depression-ravaged Washington State in the early 1930s improbably formed the rowing team that ended up winning the 1936 gold medal in Hitler's Berlin Olympics. Brown gained much of his data from firsthand (albeit retrospective) interviews. The book centers around Joe Rantz, a boy who in 1929 at the age of fifteen returned to his poor family's cabin in rural Washington to find his stepmother, his father, and his two stepbrothers in a running car about to leave for another state. He asked, "What's up, Pop? Where are we going?" His father responded that Joe was being left behind ("You are pretty much all grown up anyway"). When Joe said, "But can't I just come along?" his father said, "No. That won't work. Look, Son, if there is one thing I've figured out about life, it's that if you want to be happy, you have to learn how to be happy on your own" (p. 58).

Talk about "freedom to"! Joe did learn to fend entirely for himself—stoically alone, says Brown. The book is a long story, mostly of the trials and tribulations of a boy with "shattered self-regard." Joe did take up rowing and certainly had the strength and physique to become a powerful individual performer. To use Pink's terms (as discussed in chapter 1), he had his autonomy, growing mastery, and a sense of purpose and they took him far, but not all the way by themselves.

In a revealing, idealistic passage, Brown writes:

> The team effort—the perfectly synchronized flow of muscle, oars, boat, and water; the single, whole, unified, and beautiful symphony that a crew in motion becomes—is all that matters. Not the individual, not the self. The psychology is complex. Even as rowers must subsume their often fierce sense of independence and self-reliance, at the same time they must hold true to their individuality, their unique capabilities as oarsman . . . or, for that matter, as human beings. (2014, p. 179)

There you have it in pure form: individuality *with* connectedness.

But this picture didn't quite include Joe Rantz. He had all the self-reliance and determination in the world, but he was, understandably, a loner, suspicious of giving himself to others. Near the end of rowing trials, Joe was not on the final team— eight of the nine boys had been selected. George Pocock was a master boat builder who designed and built the racing shells for the team. He had a front row seat to see the team unfold as it practiced and competed, and noticed that Joe was not quite fitting in, even though he was bursting with individual talent.

Pocock decided to give him advice. He told Joe "that there were times when he seemed to think that he was the only fellow in the boat as if it were up to him to row the boat across the finish line all by himself" (p. 234). When a man rowed like that, said Pocock, "he was bound to attack the water rather than work with it, and worse, he was bound not to let his crew help him row" (p. 234).

Then Pocock drew his conclusion. No passage is finer than the following at capturing the tension and ultimate mutual dependence between the individual and the group:

> What mattered more than how hard a man rowed was how well everything he did in the boat harmonized with what the other fellows were doing. And a man couldn't harmonize with his crewmates unless he opened his heart to them. He had to care about his crew. It wasn't just the rowing but his crewmates that he had to give himself up to. "If you don't like some fellow in the boat, Joe, you have to learn to like him. It has to matter to you whether he wins the race, not just whether you do . . . Joe, when you really start trusting those other boys, you will feel a power at work within you that is far beyond anything you've ever imagined. Sometimes you will feel as if you have

rowed right off the planet and are rowing among the stars." (Brown, 2014, p. 235)

As Brown unfolds the story, he notes that probably nothing was more frightening to Joe than allowing himself to depend on others. But Joe did take the message that trust was at the heart of what Pocock was saying. According to Brown (presumably learned in his interview with Rantz), Joe's feelings began to shift to the point that "there was a kind of absolute truth in [Pocock's advice], something he [Joe] needed to come to terms with" (2014, p. 237).

Ultimately Joe did make the ninth spot, and the team won the gold medal (despite its coxswain passing out from illness during part of the race); they won by six-tenths of a second over the Italian boat, and one second ahead of the Germans— admittedly a Hollywood ending, but one that clearly reveals the deep relationship between self and others in service of a great cause.

Group Perspectives on Individuals

We see another revealing relationship between groups and individuals in a recent study of the Honda car company. Its author, Jeffrey Rothfeder (2014), an award-winning journalist and former editor of the *International Business Times*, finds that Honda yields more lessons for success than does its more famously studied archrival, Toyota.

Honda was founded in 1949 by Soichoro Honda, a motor-cycle machinist tinkerer. Since then, Honda has never posted a loss in its history, with profits topping 5 percent or more year after year. Its management philosophy, in contrast to Toyota's, aligns much more closely to our "freedom to" principles: innovation, satisfied workers, productivity. Note the congruence with my argument when Rothfeder identifies some of Honda's core values:

1. Individual responsibility over corporate mandates;

2. Simplicity over complexity;

3. A flat organization over an exploding flow chart;

4. Autonomous development . . . and manufacturing teams that are continuously accountable to one another;

5. Unyielding cynicism about what is believed to be the truth;

6. Decision making based on observed and verifiable facts.

Source: Rothfeder, 2014, p. 9.

In talking about individual responsibility, Rothfeder refers to Honda's underlying principle as "respect individualism." There is a clear two-way street between individual development and group performance, as the following quote illustrates:

Honda views collaboration from the vantage point of the individual, not the team. As the automaker sees it, the individual is more vital than the group; his or her capabilities, decision making, knowledge, and creativity are wellsprings from which the group's performance ultimately emerges . . . Honda's belief is that the organizational structure must serve to maximize the aptitude and skills of each individual; in turn the team, the organization, will benefit. (Rothfeder, 2014, p. 133)

In short, Honda succeeds with multinational plants all over the world, partly because it values the dynamic creative tension between individual autonomy and organizational cooperation.

Another case, drawn from education, provides some revealing lessons about the relationship between autonomy and collaboration. The history of the teaching profession is grounded in the autonomy of the classroom (too much autonomy, in my opinion). Being behind the classroom door, in your own world, means two things: you have a license to be creative and a license to be ineffective! If you are creative and isolated, your ideas do not circulate and do not benefit from feedback. If you are ineffective, you may not know how bad you really are and, in any case, do not get help. Policymakers then tighten standards and appraisal, only to lose further ground. This ends with the worst of both worlds: reduced commitment and less innovation, with no improvement in performance.

We are seeing this struggle to combine autonomy and accountability play itself out around the world. Several jurisdictions—England, states in Australia, charter schools in the United States, Sweden, and elsewhere—are granting schools "independent status" freer from traditional bureaucracies. The results are predictable: pockets of innovation among a larger number of pockets of failure. In other words, policymakers miss the point that for success you need to combine flexibility (degrees of autonomy) with requirements for cooperation.

My colleagues and I recently coined the phrase *connected autonomy* to express our view of the solution. Several jurisdictions are beginning to go down this path—giving more autonomy in exchange for commitments to cooperate. Basically the strategy is this: schools will have more autonomy in exchange for committing to three forms of cooperation— building collaborative cultures within schools, participating in networks of schools or districts to learn from each other, and relating to state policies and priorities. Connected autonomy: degrees of freedom for creativity and innovative solutions in exchange for learning from and contributing to the growth of others.

Countless instances show that collaborative schools (in which leaders help teachers focus together on improving the learning of all students) get better results and have more engaged and satisfied teachers and students. The same holds for collaborative districts: when schools and district leadership work together, and when schools network to learn from each other, all schools do well. When individuals are left on their own—even when they have the freedom of "site-based management"—they do not fare as well (see Rincon-Gallardo & Fullan, 2015). Andy Hargreaves and I have developed the case even further in our book *Professional Capital* (2012), which posits three forms of capital: human, social, and decisional. Human capital concerns the quality of individuals; social capital concerns the quality of the group working together; and decisional capital concerns how groups develop expertise. Integrating human and social capital is the answer, as people in turn develop their decision-making expertise relative to problems they need to solve.

In *Uplifting Leadership* (2014), Hargreaves and his colleagues Alan Boyle and Alma Harris went on to study how exceptionally high performing organizations across business, sports, and education sectors achieve their great results. Being good simplexity researchers, they boiled down their findings to six leadership characteristics:

1. Dreaming with determination
2. Creativity and counter-flow
3. Collaboration and competition
4. Pushing and pulling
5. Measuring with meaning
6. Sustainable success

It's mainly number 3 that is of interest to us in this chapter. Hargreaves et al. found that the high-performing systems all used collaboration within their organizations to mobilize individual and collective action relative to new destinations, greater creativity, pushing and pulling each other forward, marking and improving progress, and building in conditions for sustainability. They discuss this in such diverse cases as the reincarnation of the automaker Fiat; in the start-up microbrewer Dogfish Head Craft Brewery in the United States; in the tough inner London boroughs of Hackney and Tower Hamlets; as well in the small town of Burnley, England, and its football club.

Several of these organizations made a virtue out of friendly collaboration with their competitors. Being open with ideas, teaming up to do something neither party could do on its own, and leveraging motivational value "through the energizing thrill that people get from outdoing each other and from improving their own performance along the away" (Hargreaves et al., 2014, p. 71).

The word *uplifting* has a "freedom to" ring about it, and Hargreaves et al. invest it with three interlocking meanings:

emotional and spiritual uplift, social and moral justice, and improved performance. All three are motivational forces for individuals and for the group congruent with the ideas in this chapter.

On Struggling Alone

One question that I asked the "select dozen" practitioners I mentioned in chapter 1 was this: Can you think of a time when a principal or teacher struggled alone with a problem that needed to be dealt with by a broader group? Examples sprung to mind for all respondents along the same lines as these two:

> Yes, many of my principals over the years struggled alone. As a superintendent, I saw my role as brokering connections so that no one had to learn on their own—many challenges faced by one principal had already been worked through by a different principal. By brokering, I not only strengthened our learning organization but also developed a culture that after a while no longer needed me to do this brokering.
>
> —*Superintendent*

> Building positive teams with teacher groups can be tricky. So many personalities, philosophies, passions, etc. One teacher that stands out is a very active member of our teacher association. She almost always disagrees just to disagree. The "battle" began the minute I arrived six years ago. She would only do what the district directive was, regardless of what the data showed. The problem was that I had a team of eight teachers, and she was the only one who wanted to isolate herself. I knew I had to rely on the strength of the team to move forward. I would meet with the team chair and this teacher and discuss how she could become part of the team in a way that would improve her success. As of today she is an active

member of the team. It took about two years for her to let her guard down, but now she is active in every way. An amazing success story, actually. I think the group, and evidence that the process is working, caused her to change.

—*Elementary school principal*

Is the latter an example of inappropriate group pressure? Was this recalcitrant teacher innovative in other ways that were missed by the group? The nature of "freedom to" dynamics, such as the tension between the individual and the group, should always be a subject for reflection and worry.

The Danger of Groupthink and the Value of Solitude

Now that we appreciate cooperation more fully, let's self-correct by going back to autonomy as a positive force. The group can be not only powerful but also powerfully wrong. Janis Irving, a research psychologist at Yale and UC Berkeley, coined the term *groupthink* to describe situations where groups are cohesive, have highly directive leadership, and fail to seek external information (Irving, 1982). Such groups strive for unanimity, failing to consider alternative courses of action. In the big picture, the Bay of Pigs debacle, the *Challenger* space shuttle disaster, Hitler, terrorist groups, and religious cults come to mind.

Those of us who took Psychology 101 in college know that it's not only big-picture lapses or the groups we are in that can mislead us; complete strangers can also steer us entirely wrong, even over trivial matters. Many of us studied Asch's famous conformity experiments (1951). In one of the better-known experiments, participants were to judge which of three lines was the longest. Unbeknownst to these randomly selected play-ers, the room was sometimes also infested by a group of actors who had been prepped to unanimously give the wrong answer with confidence. In an experimental group with no actors, 99 percent of those participating got the correct answer (which was pretty obvious to the naked eye). In the group with actors, only 25 percent selected the correct response. In variations on the experiment, the proportion selecting the obviously wrong response never went below one-third.

These examples, whether big picture or small, with close team members or strangers, involved *blatant* mistakes and errors in judgment. Imagine the many more subtle ways we go along with the group without thinking about it. Groupthink is a human condition for which autonomy or a healthy psychologi-cal distance from the group is necessary medicine.

Even more interesting to me are the virtues of solitude that English psychiatrist Anthony Storr identified a quarter century ago. Clearly worried that we were going overboard in celebrat-ing the group, Storr began his analysis saying, "It seems to me that what goes on in the human being when he is by himself is as important as what happens in his interactions with other people" (1989, p. xiv).

Storr notes that "the capacity to be alone [is] linked with self-discovery and self-realization; with becoming aware of one's deepest needs, feelings, and impulses" (1989, p. 21). He claims that getting in touch with your deeper needs sometimes requires "time, passivity, and preferably solitude" (p. 26). Think of the value of meditation.

Storr found that solitude is particularly essential for imagination and creativity. The capacity to be alone facilitates "learning, thinking, innovation, coming to terms with change, and the maintenance of contact with the inner world of the imagination" (1989, p. 202).

Walter Isaacson (2014) offers a contrasting view of creativity in his most recent book, *The Innovators*. It traces the history of the computer and Internet from 1843 to the present. Isaacson makes a convincing case that "most of the innovations of the digital age were done collaboratively" (p. 1). His sweeping narrative is about how these particular innovators "collaborated and why their ability to work in teams made them even *more* creative" (p. 1, italics in original). The ideas of some of the most original innovators who remained loners failed to go anywhere—not for the obvious reason that they lacked sponsors but because, more fundamentally, they needed the creative ideas of others in the field to build on their initial insights.

Storr's and Isaacson's views appear to be in conflict, but in fact are compatible with the argument in this chapter. People need to be unencumbered by the group as they reflect on inner thoughts and ideas, but they also need the group if their ideas are to be further developed and disseminated. Groups correspondingly need individual ideas and at times the solidarity of group effort. We do not have to choose between autonomy and cooperation—*we need both*. We need to practice cycling in and out of solitude and collaboration, being careful not to overdo either.

Six Suggestions for Managers (and Others)

For organizations, jettisoning dysfunctional procedures and requirements is the way to go, but what will replace these that will better accomplish the goals of the organization and the individuals within it? Morieux and Tollman (2014), the authors who documented the growing increase of complicated layers in organizations over the past fifty years, recommend "smart simplicity," which is another term for simplexity. They spell out "six simple rules"—six factors—that strike me as entirely compatible with the four I've chosen for freedom to change:

1. Understand what your people do (what people actually do and why they do it).

2. Reinforce integrators (giving people the power and resources to foster cooperation).

3. Increase the total quantity of power by giving individuals more autonomy (create new power that serves multiple goals).

4. Increase reciprocity (objectives that reduce monopolies and increase cooperation).

5. Extend the shadow of the future (direct feedback loops that push into the future).

6. Reward those who cooperate (making transparency, innovation, and ambitious aspirations the best choices).

Source: Adapted from Morieux and Tollman, 2014, pp. 17–18.

Morieux and Tollman (2014) are primarily interested in leadership for organizations, whereas I am holding forth for both individuals and groups, but our conclusions are encouragingly similar. And you can see how even people not in formal leadership positions can do much the same as Morieux and Tollman suggest. They note that the first three rules favor the individual, and the last three rules relate to how progress plays out within the organization. Essentially, they're suggesting another way to think about balancing autonomy and cooperation. As they state: "Simple rules four, five and six are designed to impel people to confront complexity and to use their autonomy to cooperate *with* others" (p. 19, italics in original).

In short, every version of effective simplicity reduces complicatedness by focusing on how autonomy and cooperation intersect. In *Professional Capital*, Andy Hargreaves and I (2012) recommended that people need to use the group to change the group. In other words, the group should leverage people's relationships, and individuals should leverage the group. The idea that organizations and societies benefit when an individual has a degree of autonomy (and thereby has independent thoughts), along with connectedness (so that these ideas contribute to the greater good) addresses Fromm's dilemma where either isolation or absorption by the group is harmful. You don't choose the individual over the group or vice versa; as I concluded earlier, *you choose both.*

Social Media—a Final Thought

The ubiquitous and ever-growing presence of social media makes it all the more important to get the balance of autonomy and cooperation right. One can argue either way about whether digital is good or bad for humanity, but I prefer a different proactive stance. Some years ago in our change work, we drew the conclusion that if a powerful phenomenon is going to sweep you up one way or the other, you'd better try to turn the tables and move toward the danger. This is how I feel about social media.

One of the more stimulating treatments of this new world is contained in the book *Social Physics: How Good Ideas Spread,* by MIT's media lab star, Sandy Pentland (2014). Pentland is a fan of big data—the new ubiquitous data now available about all aspects of human life. Extracting patterns from massive databases is called "reality mining." We don't need to delve into the particular analyses to accept Pentland's main premise that most advances are caused through *social learning*: "a fundamental assumption is that learning from examples of other people's behavior (and the relevant contextual features) is a major and likely dominant mechanism of behavior change in humans" (p. 16).

He believes that "providing social network incentives to change 'idea flow' is a far more powerful method of changing behavior than the traditional method of using individual incentives" (2014, p. 55). I mention Pentland mainly to make the point that the social media flow of ideas and opportunities for individual and social learning will continue to expand exponentially. The message for us: we will need all our autonomous and cooperative wits about us to survive in, let alone take advantage of, the world we are becoming.

Take Action

This chapter leads to some questions that you should ask yourself:

☐ What do I do to get away from the group to reflect on and get in touch with my own inner thoughts?

☐ Are there areas in which I ought to and could be acting more autonomously than I am right now? Why am I holding back?

☐ What am I doing to cooperate with significant individuals or groups that I am connected with, in ways that contribute to both the groups and myself?

☐ What payoffs do I see from that cooperation?

☐ Right now, is there some area of my work in which I notice a lack of cooperation, either on something I want to see happen or something others have spoken about?

☐ With whom among my team or peers should I be talking more about mutual cooperation?

Next

Remember that it is not the additive contribution of autonomy and cooperation that makes the difference in freedom to change, but rather their dynamic interaction. Autonomy, getting in touch with your inner self and situation, generates ideas and insights unencumbered by the group, and allows you to process information that you are getting from the group. Cooperation refines those ideas through joint problem solving, which helps ascertain what works in practice. Now that we understand the relationship between autonomy and cooperation, it should not be hard to see why feedback is our next topic.

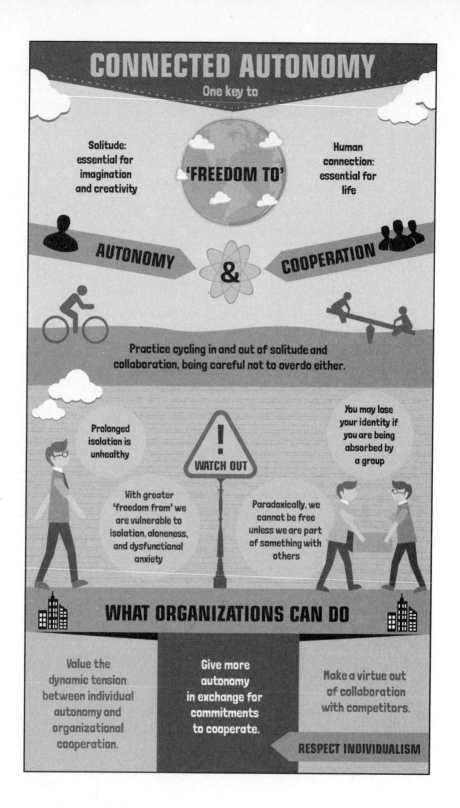

CHAPTER · FOUR

Feedback

Everything that irritates us about others can lead us to an understanding of ourselves.

—Carl Jung

I f you're going to enjoy being autonomous and cooperating, you need to get better at doing both. Seeking feedback and managing unsolicited feedback offer a gold mine of potential growth. But mining gold is hard work; mastering the art of feedback is extremely difficult, too. Even understanding its challenge is hard, so let me lay out my general argument in advance.

1. **People don't like feedback and want to be free from it.**
   Why? One reason is that it's painful to the ego and hard to understand correctly. A second reason is that it's often given as a way to discipline rather than inform, serving to demoralize and demotivate.

2. **Feedback is one of the key interacting simplifiers for individuals and groups wanting to change.** It should be something we actively ("freely") seek.

3. **To think in terms of active seeking means to think first and foremost in terms of what *receivers* of feedback need and can do,** rather than from the perspective of the person who is giving feedback. For this tactic of simplexity, we take a cue from a book by Douglas Stone and Sheila Heen (2014) of Harvard Law School, *Thanks for Feedback: The Science and Art of Receiving Feedback Well.* Make the center of gravity the *receiver,* not the giver.

4. **Giving and taking feedback are both challenging,** but five basic factors work in combination. Whether you are

giver or receiver, think about these: inspiring purpose, the quality of interaction, good and transparent data, candor infused with a developmental purpose, and respect for the receiver's autonomy.

So in this chapter, first and primarily, we are going to turn feedback on its head, unmoor it from formal appraisal procedures, and ask simply how we can learn more by paying attention to cues pertaining to how well we are doing and how we can improve. How can individuals develop their own feedback with others above, below, and beside them? How can you as an individual increase your ability to *receive and indeed seek* feedback, whether it is informal (in your daily interactions within the culture) or more formal (appraisal)? Oddly, there is not much research on how to receive or otherwise pick up feedback, but there are some useful ideas.

Secondarily, how can top people in the organization exploit feedback in making their reports more effective? I will include advice on this matter. This should lead us to a few highlights on how organizations can establish conditions conducive to continuous learning. (After all, this must be the meaning of the elusive "learning organization.")

It may not seem fair to place the burden on the receiver, but at the end of the day, do you want to be right, or do you want to grow? I am reminded of Carrie Fisher's observation that "resentment is like taking poison and waiting for the other person to die" (cited in Huffington, 2014, p. 121). It is your life, not theirs, that you want to improve. If you ignore feedback altogether because it is delivered ineptly or superficially, you shut down avenues of potential insight. That is why I say that the responsibility for learning from feedback rests with the receiver, not the giver.

Your job as receiver is to seek and sort out feedback, because feedback is too important to your growth for you to wait until the giver gets more skilled at delivering it. Receive it undistorted, warts and all, and work at what you can learn.

The Beast of Distortion

Think specifically about yourself and ask, "What have I learned over the last couple of years arising from feedback I was given or that I picked up?" Consider others you live or work with most closely and ask what they have learned from feedback, whether it came from you or not. Be careful here—you may be biased in favor of yourself: "Why do you look at the speck in your brother's eye, but do not notice the log that is in your own eye?" (Matthew 7:3).

So enters one form of distortion, *the* central challenge of receiving feedback. Distortion stems from a conundrum we all face as humans: we want to learn, we want to be liked, and we want to like ourselves; but these three desires don't sit well together. Inevitably, they give rise to serious warping.

As Stone and Heen (2014) put it, "Receiving feedback sits at the intersection of . . . two needs—our drive to learn and our need for acceptance" (p. 8). And most of us have a higher opinion of ourselves than others do of us. (From our leadership work, I would say that the higher up you go in an organization, the greater the self-deception.) For example, 90 percent of managers believe that their performance in the workplace is in the top 10 percent, and 93 percent of American motorists believe that they are better-than-average drivers (Stone & Heen, p. 64). At the same time, Stone and Heen note, "We judge ourselves by our intentions, while others judge us by our impact" (p. 88).

More distortion arises because the motives behind what others say of us are often hard to discern, and people may not be clear themselves about why they are saying certain things. You can't be sure where they are coming from—was that supposed to be a helpful comment, or was it a dig? (Just because you are paranoid doesn't mean that the person is not out to get you.)

In short, you are living in a world of distorting mirrors, but you can learn how to correct for those distortions. Instead of trying to figure out the motives underlying the range of direct and indirect feedback you get in the course of the week (an exhausting and low-yield proposition), focus back on yourself as receiver and what it is you are trying to learn about yourself.

I asked our select dozen lead practitioners a couple of questions on feedback: "What's some painful feedback you received, and how did you go about accepting and using it well?" Here are some of the responses:

> As superintendent, I would get a great deal of feedback. When I got feedback that was extremely critical, I always tried to find something I could react to affirmatively and use as a lesson to go forward.
>
> —*Superintendent*

Another superintendent referred to the time he was a young teacher:

> Receiving no feedback is very difficult. It left me feeling unsure. It began to impact my self-confidence. My performance began to suffer because I was not sure how to proceed; and when I

did proceed, it felt as if I may not be moving in the correct direction . . . Again, this was all my perception because nothing was said. In the end, it actually paralyzed me, and I chose to leave that school and landed with a much different principal.

This same person, who went on to become chief superintendent of a large district, talked about how he learned to receive feedback:

I work hard to listen well, when my first inclination might be to respond defensively. I focus on understanding others' perspectives and ask for clarity if I am unclear.

—Superintendent

Receiving no feedback or superficial feedback can be a bit deflating, but sometimes we must pull our own happiness wagon. I have like others received demotivating feedback. It might take a bit of time, but that too can be used as self-motivation to move forward.

—Secondary school principal

I remember meeting a student I had taught several years later, and she proudly claimed that she had made it. She said she had been successful in spite of me. I took that message quite hard because I see myself as a strong advocate of students. The incident reminded me how powerful it is to be a teacher, and you always have to be careful about how you treat your student.

—Superintendent

Painful feedback is still feedback, and it needs to be used to improve the situation. Last school year, I had our annual fireside chat with teachers and staff at the school. Well, one teacher decided it would be a good time to give all the feedback necessary to turn the school into a much better learning and teaching environment. He gave me his feedback, which was: "Be more reliable; if a time and date are set, stick to it; more team planning is needed so we can get the work done; there are too many teachers who don't want to teach in the classroom." I took this feedback into the school year and made some changes. What I learned from this is: try and get more regular feedback before a teacher feels mounting frustration. And what I have learned about painful feedback is that there is usually a valid reason to be delivered.

—Elementary school principal

Sometimes our perceived strengths can be our weaknesses:

My most painful feedback was when I was a teacher trying to become a teacher leader. I was told my "passion" came across as negative or in some cases like a bully. I was shocked! This was holding me back, and I knew I had to change. Although I knew I wasn't a bully, I also knew that I had to change the perception others had of me. I volunteered for every leadership opportunity possible. I asked my supervisors for feedback in group situations. Overall it turned out OK. Now my passions are looked at as passions.

—Elementary school principal

I chose to consult these individuals because I know they are (they became) effective at their work. They are learners under all circumstances. They turned feedback to their advantage. That is what you need to strive for as well.

Stop Doing What Doesn't Work

Besides focusing on the receiver and acknowledging distortion, another ingredient of simplexity in handling feedback is simply to stop doing what doesn't work and is a waste of time.

Sometimes feedback is too vague to be helpful. At other times feedback devolves into nothing more than a tool for justifying punishments and rewards for people under our control. At other times its main effect is simply to discourage and demotivate any change at all. The net result is that people increasingly close themselves off from feedback. When formal feedback doesn't work—and that's true most of the time—leaders either give up (play the game) or push harder (be more and more blunt and consequential). In either case, feedback fails to make a difference. It's "interesting," Stone and Heen wryly observe, that both givers and receivers often simply back off taking responsibility for failed formal feedback: "When we give feedback, we notice that the receiver isn't good at receiving it. When we receive feedback, we notice that the giver isn't good at giving it" (2014, p. 3).

Stone and Heen (2014) give other examples of useless or counterproductive feedback:

> Margie receives a "meets expectations," which sounds to her like "really, you still work here?" . . .
>
> Rodrigo reads over his 360-degree feedback report. Repeatedly. He can't make head nor tail out of it, but one thing has changed: He now feels awkward with his colleagues, all 360 degrees of them . . .
>
> Your spouse has been complaining about your character flaws for years. You think of this less as your spouse "giving you feedback" and more as "being annoying." (p. 2)

Increased surveillance and other forms of tightening the screws are easily deflected by those on the receiving end. Hargreaves, Boyle, and Harris (2014) devote almost ten pages to what they call "dark data" usage. My favorite example (although there are others that are downright criminal involving fudging the books for financial gain) comes from World Cup soccer. Professional sports teams use data these days as a matter of course. One feedback strategy was based on how much energy players seemed to expend during the course of the game. Some teams started to place microchips in players' boots to gather data about the number of steps players took during the game as a proxy measure for expended energy. Some established "step targets," only to find that players began to take rapid baby steps when there was a stoppage of play and they were out of sight of cameras. Humans do not like to be monitored in ways they perceive as insulting or degrading. Employees have more ways to outwit managers than managers have to increase surveillance. And even if you catch people doing the wrong thing, doing so doesn't motivate them or even help them figure out how to do their work more effectively.

We have already seen from large-scale surveys that less than a third of employees are engaged at work. Sisodia, Wolfe, and Sheth (2007) report that only 13.8 percent of respondents said that their organization had an "enthusiastic workforce." Lack of feedback, or the presence of wrong forms of feedback, have compounded the problem, driving workers further away. When people are left alone—unsupervised if you like—or when they are monitored through formal appraisal, their work does not improve.

Recasting Feedback

We don't have that many tools available to help us in the "freedom to" world. If we recast its role, feedback can become one of the most powerful forces for the betterment of the individual and the organization.

The previous chapter on combining autonomy and cooperation paved the way to understanding how feedback can be built into our simplexity solution for freedom to change. We know that autonomy and cooperation together help. If feedback infuses the interplay of the two, it strengthens the value of both.

As I've already suggested, recast feedback in your life and work as something you actively seek. As with every other path to change, don't wait for the organization to get it right. Learning is in the eye (and control) of the recipient. From the time we are born, we like to learn, but "learning *about* ourselves is a whole new ballgame" (Stone & Heen, 2014, pp. 6–7, italics in original).

You can always be in charge of how and whether you accept the content of the feedback, but you have to put yourself in a position to receive, which at the beginning will feel like putting yourself in harm's way. If you have to decide whether to err on the side of being worried about acceptance versus the side of learning, choose learning. Once you get past the initial fear of seeking feedback, you will gain on both the learning and acceptance counts:

> The bold-faced benefits of seeking feedback are: Our relationships are richer, our self-esteem more secure, and, of course, we learn—we get better at things and feel good about that . . . And . . . when we get good at receiving feedback even our toughest opponents come to feel a little less threatening. (Stone & Heen, 2014, pp. 8, 9)

The outcomes, in short, tend to be on the positive side (all the more attractive when we consider the negative things that we have warded off—lack of engagement, bad relationships with peers and bosses, and the like). Stone and Heen report that feedback-seeking behavior has been linked to job satisfaction, greater creativity on the job, and lower turnover. Marriage benefits, too, as research from John Gottman found that "a person's willingness and ability to accept influence and input from their spouse is a key predictor of a healthy stable marriage" (cited in Stone & Heen, 2014, p. 9).

The advice is clear: take a risk and seek feedback, both because you will be worse off if you do nothing and because you will learn from it.

Think about these questions:

1. Are you already getting feedback, and it's simply too much? Narrow down your own priorities about what types of things you most want or need feedback about. Turn them into a short list you can use to focus your own attention and to help your givers be more helpful.

2. When you give feedback, train yourself to think of the receiver. What might be his or her state of mind? Focus on the clarity of the message, not on how you can convince the person to take the feedback.

Enhance Your Work Culture

Beyond improving how you handle feedback, you can be proactive by sizing up the kind of organizational culture you work in. What you want to look for and maybe even help tweak is a culture that values, invests in, and cultivates five qualities (not that all will be present):

1. An overarching and inspiring sense of purpose

2. Quality interaction: camaraderie and peer motivation relative to the work (we saw in chapter 1 that this was the number-one positive factor, according to worker surveys)

3. Good, transparent data

4. Candor of feedback infused with a developmental purpose

5. Respect for autonomy

Cultures with these five characteristics generate a lot of feedback and, at the same time, maximize the possibility that the receiver of feedback will learn from it.

An Inspiring Purpose

Hargreaves et al. (2014) studied high-performing organizations in three sectors and found that a key feature of these groups was that they were inspired by "dreaming with determination." The dreams were lofty but specific, promising to bring people to a different place. For example, in the initially low-performing, diverse, high-poverty boroughs of Hackney and Tower Hamlets (which I have also studied) in London, England, the goal was that parents would fight to get their children into its schools (whereas at the starting point, many parents wanted to transfer their children out of those schools). The dream was that poverty would not be an acceptable excuse for failure. Ten years later, both Hackney and Tower Hamlets had become two of the highest-performing local authorities in England. That kind of dream and drive can make you want to get up in the morning and get going.

Quality Interaction

Concerning camaraderie and quality interaction, we have already seen in chapter 3 that a great deal of learning goes on when people collaborate and learn from each other. Purposeful interaction contains valuable, ongoing feedback. Even though it appears to be informal, such feedback is powerful and pervasive because people interact around particular problems. Consider the last three of Morieux and Tollman's six "simple rules" (introduced in chapter 3), those directed at the group: increasing reciprocity, extending the shadow of the future, and rewarding those who cooperate. As the authors observe:

> The last three rules achieve [people's input to the organization] by creating feedback loops that expose people, as directly as possible, to the consequences of their actions. Some of the feedback loops are contained in tasks and activities, rather than imposed from outside, so they have an immediate effect on people—either gratifying or penalizing—depending on how much good they do in their current work situations . . . [T]he loops tailor themselves to specific circumstances. (2014, p. 110)

Transparent Data

Good, transparent data adds specificity to the interaction. Morieux and Tollman (2014) talk about strengthening the quality of feedback loops by increasing the frequency with which people review collective results. However, the use of data—so massively more available in the digital age—remains a challenge. Hargreaves et al. (2014) found that their "uplifting organizations" paid attention to what the authors labeled "measurement with meaning." They found that what distinguishes uplifting organizations is not that they are data driven but "how they *define and draw* on the data that are important to them" (p. 113, italics in original). Such organizations use data to determine how well they are progressing, what's working and why, and what needs to be done for improvement. They monitor results and practices. They have a culture of transparency that draws on the individual and collective energy of the members of the organization to focus on development and improvement. To put it in our terms, they have a culture of autonomy and cooperation with a purpose and focus.

Hargreaves et al. (2014) found, as we did in our own work with effective school districts and systems, that successful organizations establish a clear focus, give feedback about impact and progress, and intervene with coaching and capacity building (see Fullan & Quinn, 2015, where we show how school districts get better results through "coherence," defined as focused direction, collaborating, deepening learning, and data-based accountability). These organizations "use *meaningful metrics* that connect indicators to core purposes, and that value personal experience and relationships alongside objective evidence as a basis for judgment" (Hargreaves et al., p. 134, italics in original). Under these circumstances, they are able to set stretch targets with employees. People rise to the occasion when they are participating in something meaningful and have a way of influencing and measuring progress. The absence of good data on progress (or lack thereof)—a kind of "freedom from" no-man's-land—is deadly. Patrick Lencioni (2007) named this state as one of "three signs of a miserable job." He called this the problem of "immeasurement." He found that people wanted to know whether and how their contribution made a difference.

> Employees need to be able to gauge their progress and level of contribution for themselves. They cannot be fulfilled in their work if their success depends on the opinions or whims of another person, no matter how benevolent that person may be. Without a tangible means of assessing success or failure, motivation eventually deteriorates as people see themselves as unable to control their own fate. (Lencioni, 2007, p. 222)

Incidentally, the other two signs of a miserable job are anonymity (nobody knows my name or cares), and irrelevance (I am just a cog in the machine).

Candor and Respect for Autonomy

Assessing success and failure *is* feedback. It is essential for further success, but only if there are motivating circumstances and mechanisms for acting on the feedback. The likelihood that the feedback will be acted on is a function of the final two components of feedback: candor, and respect for autonomy. This is a very sophisticated set to get right because of ever-critical interaction effects.

To examine the candor-autonomy duo, I am going to shift from talking about how individuals can seek feedback to how organizations might get the conditions right in the first place, by taking up the remarkable story of Pixar, the wildly successful animated film movie studio.

, , ,

Ed Catmull is the CEO and president of Pixar Animation and Disney Animation. His book, *Creativity, Inc.: Overcoming the Unseen Forces That Stand in the Way of True Inspiration* (2014), is an insightful account of Pixar's journey. The big question that Catmull takes up is how Pixar was able to make fourteen blockbuster animated movies in a row (starting with *Toy Story* and ending with *Monsters University*) in a highly competitive and creative industry. The backstory is interesting to note briefly: Catmull and a couple of his colleagues were young pioneering engineers who were among the first to develop computer-generated animation. The group was first bought by George Lucas, then by Steve Jobs when he was head of NeXT; finally, Jobs sold Pixar to Disney, a deal in which Jobs and Catmull negotiated autonomy for Pixar within Disney.

Catmull seems to be rare among CEOs in his preoccupation with, and introspection about, what makes an effective company. By being reflective and deliberate about what makes for a great organization—in effect setting up his own feedback system—he learned a great deal about the nature of highly creative organizations, going from practice to theory if you like. His book uncovers many of the themes of effective feedback that we have been considering. This should sound familiar:

> I've spent nearly forty years thinking about how to help smart, ambitious people work effectively with one another . . . I believe that managers must loosen controls, not tighten them. They must accept risk; they must trust people they work with and strive to clear the path for them, and always, they must pay attention to and engage anything that creates fear. (pp. xv–xvi)

But what did Catmull do to ensure that this was not just a case of aimless "freedom to"? The heart of the feedback system at Pixar is based on establishing a culture that explicitly embraces "honesty and candor combined with autonomy" (p. 87). The phrase acknowledges the fantastic interaction effects that obtain when candor is valued along with a fair degree of autonomy with respect to whether or not the recipient actually takes the advice. Assuming you and I have agreed on the ground rules, if I give you good, direct feedback on a particular matter *and* we have agreed that you can take it or leave it, paradoxically you are more likely to take the feedback into account. The burden of proof for action is on you, the receiver, not me, the giver. In this way, we have finessed the problem of my failing to give any good feedback (leaving you in a vacuum), or my giving you feedback that you don't welcome (and therefore will fail to act on). You can, in other words, have your feedback and eat it, too. (Thank you, editor, for letting this pun survive the editing process.)

Feedback is crucial for learning, but many obstacles stand in its way. This is why we need to be explicit about the feedback process and about the conditions under which it is to be given, received, and potentially acted on. This is exactly what Catmull and his group did. For the sake of candor, Pixar established the Braintrust, a group of peers who meet every few months or so to assess each movie as it is being made. As Catmull put it: "Put smart, passionate people in a room together, and charge them with identifying and solving problems, and encourage them to be candid with each other" (2014, p. 87). Pixar learned how crucial the Braintrust was, "Because, early on, *all* of our movies suck" (p. 90, italics in original). In any complex endeavor, early versions will almost certainly be deficient. This is normal. Feedback is fortune because it is essential for improvement, especially in early phases of the work.

The autonomy part is equally crucial. The Braintrust watches early mock-ups of the movie and "discusses what's not ringing true, what could be better, what's not working at all" (p. 90). But: "Notably, [the Braintrust] do not *prescribe* how to fix the problems they diagnose. They test weak points, they make suggestions, but it is up to the director to settle on a path forward" (p. 90, italics in the original).

It is up to the director to settle on a path forward! Candor and autonomy coexisting: thus the Braintrust provides valuable feedback but has no authority. Catmull says that the Braintrust actually doesn't *want* to solve the problem, because in all likelihood the director and his or her creative team will come up with a better solution, once they get good feedback. "We raise our game not be being prescriptive but by offering candor and deep analysis" (p. 93).

More insights from Catmull:

> To set up a healthy feedback system, you must remove the power dynamics from the equation—you must enable yourself, in other words, to focus on the problem, not the person . . .

> Candor isn't cruel. It does not destroy. On the contrary, any successful feedback is built on empathy, in the idea that we are all on this together, that we understand your pain because we've experienced it ourselves. (pp. 94, 104)

Once again we see autonomy and cooperation. It is not as if no tough decisions are made. Over the years, two movies were halted and the directors replaced. Another film, after three years of development, proved to be so "confounding that we shut it down altogether" (2014, p. 107).

If candor, trust, and autonomy are the norm, and it nearly always works out for the better, people begin to trust the process. Within this context, tough decisions when they are required are more likely to be taken and to be accepted. This puts the idea of failure in a whole new light. Problems are a result of doing something new. They are normal to learning and exploration. With a learning/feedback culture, problem solving is maximized during the process. People innovate (take risks) knowing that they can learn as they go. Says Catmull, "Management's job is not to prevent risk, but to build the ability to recover" (2014, p. 128).

"Freedom to," to pick up our earlier theme from Eric Fromm, is accompanied by isolation, fear, loneliness, and anxiety. You either grow or die. Catmull understands this: "Candor, safety, research, self-assessment and protecting the new are all mechanisms we can use to confront the unknown and to keep the chaos and fear to a minimum" (2014, p. 185).

We are not all making Hollywood movies, but the principles are the same. Wherever you see yourself in the hierarchy of your organization, if you are going to try something new, you will by definition encounter problems. You need candid feedback from others, especially early in the process, to address those issues. Trust and autonomy to figure out the feedback are important. Candor means interaction. Interaction means influence. If you are fortunate to work for an organization like Pixar, take advantage of feedback opportunities. If not, push for feedback related to your short list of key priorities. It is up to you to make the best of the situation.

Opportunity Need Not Be Lost

To integrate the ideas in this chapter, I turn now to school systems, because they represent such an egregious example of lost opportunity when it comes to feedback. The consequences of this for students, teachers, and society are horrendous. Potentially, improvements in feedback for learning could yield huge value. Because feedback is learning, you would think that education would have a high stake in its presence. But it seems that the public school system was set up for teachers to give feedback to students (which is not done well, by the way) while handicapping any attempt to give feedback to teachers as well. Because feedback *is* learning, it should be ubiquitous in schools—the lifeblood of its culture: teacher-student; student-teacher; student-student; teacher-teacher; principal-teacher and vice versa; parent-school; and more. Sadly, this is not happening on any scale. Let's look at teachers first, then students.

Teachers, the single largest group of public employees, have a long history of being kept or staying behind the classroom door—the lonely profession, as someone has called it. This means that variations in the quality of teaching are large and unattended to. Good ideas from successful teachers fail to spread, and bad teaching practices persist. When the classroom door closes, individual teachers enter a free zone (or so it seems; ineffectiveness has its own way of enslaving us).

Ever since research discovered the dangerous half-truth that the teacher is the single most influential factor affecting learning, policymakers have taken steps to address the matter by increasingly attempting to measure and control what teachers are doing. They have developed teacher appraisal schemes and requirements that have school principals and others meeting with teachers to go over their teaching with the help of an increasingly specific checklist. Because this approach doesn't work very well to pinpoint how to improve, let alone to motivate teachers to engage in making improvements, principals and their teachers adjust by going through the motions. As I mentioned in chapter 2, in the most recent TALIS report (Organization for Economic Cooperation and Development, 2014b), almost 50 percent of teacher respondents said that their leaders conducted appraisal primarily to meet administrative requirements—that is, they went through the motions perfunctorily to meet the letter of the law.

Well, if something doesn't work, why spend precious time on it? Why let superficiality become the name of the game? In business it is the same. Stone and Heen (2014) report that giving feedback is so difficult that "avoidance is ubiquitous"; 63 percent of executives indicate that their "managers lack courage to have the difficult performance discussion," yet "lack of meaningful feedback was the number one reason cited by talented people for leaving an organization" (p. 293).

New teachers leave the profession in droves—the percentage of teachers leaving teaching in the first five years ranges from 30 to 50 percent, depending on the jurisdiction. One new teacher said, "I felt like the soldier dropped behind enemy lines with nothing more than orders" (Niver, 2013). Many promising young teachers leave because no one is helping them overcome classroom management problems or problems of overwork. Note that my criterion is very minimal here: Are teachers even showing up? Are they even staying on the job, let alone continuously improving through ongoing feedback? In the TALIS survey population, two-thirds of teachers had never observed other teachers teaching; almost 50 percent had never received feedback of any kind from their principal.

In education, some 98 percent of teachers are rated satisfactory or better; in other words, current appraisal practices obviously do not work. So policymakers have taken that half-truth—that individual teachers are key—a notch higher into "teacher evaluation" linked to performance pay, including dismissal. This makes matters worse because it creates a demotivating scenario for most people. In chapter 1 we heard from Daniel Pink that carrots and sticks have a dismal track record for all but mechanical tasks. For a system to increase the rigor of individual evaluation schemes is the psychological equivalent of scorching the whole lawn to get rid of a few weeds. The more intrusive schemes seem to be designed to get at the worst teachers while casting a pall over the entire profession.

We don't have to be stuck with this dysfunctional status quo. The choice is not between having no system or having a bad one. We actually know what works. In *The Principal*, I summarized the research on effective schools (Fullan, 2014). Essentially, when teachers team up in a focused manner, continuously sort out best teaching practices, work closely with evidence on student learning, give quality feedback to students, and learn from one another, they get results. There is a lot of natural feedback in these collaborative cultures.

As mentioned earlier, Andy Hargreaves and I (2012) have further developed the concept and practices of collaborative cultures in our book on professional capital and its three components—human, social, and decisional. This theme has been taken up further by Carrie Leanna (2011), a business professor at University of Pittsburgh who has been examining social capital for more than a decade. In a typical study, Leanna measures three things: human capital (with questions about the qualifications of teachers on staff), social capital (with questions to teachers about such topics as the extent to which they and their peers work in a collaborative, focused way to improve the learning of all students in the school), and math achievement over the course of the year.

She found that, yes, teachers with higher human capital tend to get results, but the strongest results occurred in schools with strong social capital as well. She also found that teachers with lower human capital who happened to be in a school with high social capital also got better results over the course of the year. Leanna did not examine decisional capital (how individuals and teams get better at expert decision making), but had she done so, I'm sure that she would have found even stronger results.

Within strong collaborative cultures, an enormous amount of feedback occurs naturally through daily focused interactions. Just ask yourself this: Which of the following two practices is likely to have the greater impact: teacher appraisal or a collaborative culture? Appraisal, even when it is done well (which is rare), is not powerful overall because it can never be intensive enough. It is a low-yield strategy relative to the energy required to cover the staff. I am not saying never do it—it should, for example, be used with beginning teachers; but don't count on it to carry the day for the school as a whole. Collaborative culture is the powerhouse. It faces you the moment you walk in the door, and stays with you day after day. People get natural feedback because it is built into the culture. When you are in such a culture for a while, the biggest cumulative effect is the development of *shared depth of understanding about the nature of the work.* The conclusion about feedback is: learn in context or learn superficially.

Although my colleagues and I are focused on building such collaborative cultures within and across schools by working with leaders at the school and system level, in this chapter I emphasize what you as an individual can and should do. My primary message: seek feedback, as did the elementary principal we heard from earlier, who found that her passion for helping children learn was being interpreted as bullying. Using this feedback, she joined teacher teams and asked her supervisors for feedback on whether she was coming on too strong, and she eventually became a highly successful principal in a very difficult school.

We are talking here about radical changes in the culture of the teaching profession (and, it seems, of most organizations). Opening up constructive feedback will be a difficult but powerful source of new development and satisfaction. For the most part in this chapter, I have urged individuals to take action for themselves and those around them. In *Professional Capital,* Hargreaves and I (2012) offered some guidelines for individual action:

- Start with yourself
- Examine your own behavior
- Build your human capital through social capital
- Push and pull your peers
- Invest in and accumulate your decisional capital

- Manage up by helping your leaders be the best they can be
- Take the first step
- Connect everything back to your students

Yes, but Who Is the Receiver?

Within a school, administrators and teachers are only one partner in the dance. What about the students? It seems obvious that if teachers are not getting or seeking feedback on a daily basis from others involved in the same work of improving learning, they are hardly in a position to be good at giving feedback to students. Teachers are, of course, engaged every day in giving feedback to students because that is what learning is about. But the question is: Are they good at it? Are they getting better and better at giving feedback to students?

John Hattie is a professor and director of the Melbourne Education Research Institute who for the last twenty years has been studying the impact of different instructional practices on student engagement and achievement. One of his tools is the metastudy—a study in which one identifies an outcome (such as student achievement) and a practice (such as giving students feedback) and then reviews all the research on how the practice affects the outcome, calculating the "effect size" based on the research evidence. Hattie (2009) conducted over a thousand studies, incorporating scores of individual studies into several metastudy analyses. He uncovered fascinating patterns, which he calls "visible learning."

Hattie ended up with over one hundred variables, which he rank-ordered from high to low impact on student learning.

Near the very top of Hattie's results was "feedback to students"—highly influential but also *infrequently done well*. Hattie says, "I spent many hours in classrooms [observing feedback], noting its absence, despite the claims of the best of teachers that they are constantly engaged in providing feedback" (2009, p. 173). Feedback occurred, but it was more about behavioral issues. Fellow researchers and practitioners knew that feedback was a critical variable and by and large were working on the topic of how teachers could give better feedback to students. Then Hattie had an epiphany, exactly the one we came to early in this chapter:

> The mistake I made was seeing feedback as something *teachers provided to students* . . . It was only when I discovered that feedback was most powerful when it is from the *student to the teacher* that I started to understand it better. (p. 173, italics in original)

We have come full circle. If you want to increase the power of feedback, focus on the receiver, not the giver. Where you are the giver, what can you learn from receivers about their state of mind, what they might be saying about you, and how you might construct a better learning environment?

Educational systems are ripe for action. Students, teachers, parents, administrators, and policymakers are variously bored, alienated, frustrated, and desperate. Shifting from giving no or superficial feedback to giving constructive feedback for adults and for students would open up a gold mine of improvement. I can't think of any other single factor that would yield as much payoff as unleashing the collective efficacy that would be generated by ongoing feedback. That is why my colleagues and I are tackling this problem with thousands of practitioners and students around the world under an initiative we call New Pedagogies for Deep Learning (newpedagogies.org).

We define the core of better learning as a "new learning partnership between and among teachers, students, and families." This means that learning will be revamped to include strategies to establish and combine the following constituent parts:

- Self-learning
- Peer-to-peer student learning
- Student-teacher learning
- Teacher-teacher learning

The whole set of processes will be heavily laden with multichannel, two-way feedback with respect to given educational goals and outcomes. Individuals will need to learn how to self-monitor as they give and receive feedback with peers and others below and above them. The impact on engagement of teachers and students and on their learning could be huge.

Feedback Unchained

In this chapter, we have looked at some of the answers to maximizing the presence and impact of feedback:

- Focus on the receiver
- Make it the receiver's job and opportunity to seek and sort out feedback
- Stop doing what doesn't work

- Improve the quality of interactions
- Use good data transparently
- Combine candor and autonomy

The key messages in this chapter lead to a radical reformulation of how feedback can be improved in organizations. Start with the widespread finding that the majority of workers in all organizations are not engaged and receive little effective feedback that would enable them to learn and grow. What leaders have been doing erroneously is starting with the top end of the problem—how to improve the giving of feedback—and neglecting the bottom end—how to improve learning conditions. I can't think of many more insulting actions than giving workers in a culture of disengagement feedback about how *they* should improve, when it is the organization that should improve. (This doesn't mean that the individuals should not want to improve, but more that they would be doing so for themselves as much as for the organization.) If leaders focus instead on improving the organization—what motivates people, purposeful peer interaction, collaborative cultures, more leeway or autonomy for groups, use of data and evidence for growth, and so on—they will build deeper and more sustainable feedback systems into the culture.

Let's unhitch feedback from appraisal and reposition it as the sum total of all the various forms of feedback you get as a member of an organization—and then strengthen it. I have said that regardless of the kind of culture you are in, it is in your best interest to seek feedback so that you can improve. Seek and contribute to cultures that build in feedback as part and parcel of improving the organization and the people in it.

Step back and appreciate that feedback is at the heart of personal betterment. Make your contribution for yourself and those around you.

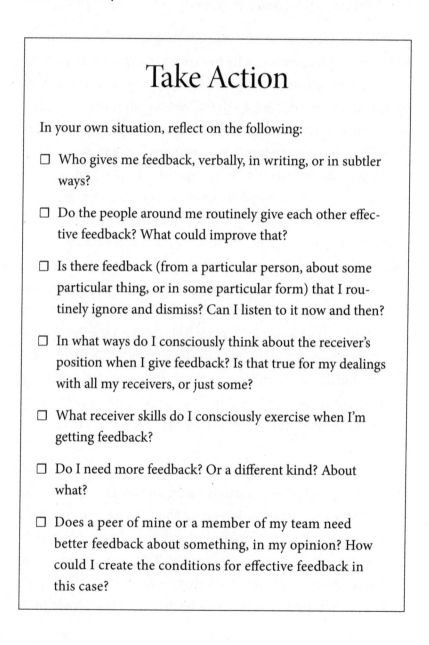

Take Action

In your own situation, reflect on the following:

☐ Who gives me feedback, verbally, in writing, or in subtler ways?

☐ Do the people around me routinely give each other effective feedback? What could improve that?

☐ Is there feedback (from a particular person, about some particular thing, or in some particular form) that I routinely ignore and dismiss? Can I listen to it now and then?

☐ In what ways do I consciously think about the receiver's position when I give feedback? Is that true for my dealings with all my receivers, or just some?

☐ What receiver skills do I consciously exercise when I'm getting feedback?

☐ Do I need more feedback? Or a different kind? About what?

☐ Does a peer of mine or a member of my team need better feedback about something, in my opinion? How could I create the conditions for effective feedback in this case?

Next

At this point we have dealt with the first two parts of our simplexity quartet, having addressed autonomy-cooperation and
feedback. The third member is accountability. What role can it
play in strengthening the first two, and how can we achieve the
right kind of accountability, given that "freedom to" does not
mean we should be free to do whatever we want?

FEEDBACK

We don't have many tools to help us in the 'freedom to' world, but feedback can become a powerful force for improvement if we recast its role.

Your goal should be how to better receive and seek feedback

People don't like feedback

We should actively seek feedback

Giving and taking feedback is challenging

Make the center of gravity the receiver not the giver

The Beast of Distortion

Distortion stems from a conundrum we all face. We want to learn, be liked, and like ourselves, but these desires don't sit well together. Inevitably, they give rise to serious warping.

97% of Americans believe they're better-than-average drivers.

Organizations should use feedback to promote continuous learning.

Be a learner under all circumstances

How to maximize the presence and impact of feedback as learning

Focus on the receiver

Make it the receiver's job to seek and sort out feedback

Stop doing what doesn't work

Improve the quality of interactions

Use good data transparently

Combine candor and autonomy

CHAPTER · FIVE

Accountability

Accountability: The quality or state of being accountable, especially an obligation or willingness to accept responsibility or to account for one's actions.

—Merriam-Webster dictionary

If you are seeking feedback and using feedback as an opportunity for you to learn with respect to important goals, you are already on the path of accountability: a willingness to accept responsibility for your own actions. Tackling accountability is a complex business. What if the organization for which you work is not doing its part? For example, suppose a novice teacher is thrown into a school where there is no culture of accountability. This teacher can't afford to quit the job on the spot, but knows the year will be hell if she gets no help from other teachers or the principal. For what should she hold herself accountable if no one is helping her see her mistakes? Is she helpless? What can she do? We will return to this example near the end of the chapter. In the meantime, I'll show how, in general, it is in your own interest to promote, together with those around you, a greater sense of responsibility—a greater accountability of the right kind.

Richard Elmore (2004), professor at the Harvard Graduate School of Education, argues that we need what he calls "reciprocity of accountability":

Accountability must be a reciprocal process. For every increment of performance I demand from you, I have an equal responsibility to provide you with the capacity to meet that expectation. Likewise, for every investment that you make in my skill and knowledge, I have a reciprocal obligation to demonstrate some new increment in performance. This is the principle of "reciprocity of accountability." (Elmore, 2004, p. 93)

Elmore's reciprocity seems just and correct in theory, but most organizations do not operate as he describes. For that reason, my advice will be to see if you can't make more progress by starting where you are, regardless of what reciprocity is or isn't raining down from above. The idea is to leverage your colleagues toward what I will call *internal accountability*, through which the individual and the group are accountable to themselves and each other and thus more able to grapple with or engage the external accountability system.

We are going to start with what unfortunately happens when systems operate from the top down, simply demanding accountability from the folks below. From there we will tweak Elmore's many insights toward a solution—answering not "How can I get my boss to act differently?" but "How can my peers and I act in a way that enhances accountability in a way that benefits us?" The "freedom to" world can't be one free of obligations; rather we must situate obligations in a way that increases our own development, that of our peers, and, in the process, that of the system.

External Accountability: Why We All Wish It Would Go Away

I take educational systems as examples of ones that, ironically, have miscast accountability in a way that *reduces* actual accountability at the individual and group level. Here is how it does so. As policymakers become increasingly frustrated at the poor performance of public schools, they become more demanding, insisting on "evaluation with teeth," such as performance pay with corresponding consequences (intervention, removing the principal, closing the school). In the meantime, teachers have grown up in a highly individualistic culture (entrenched behind the classroom door) where responsibility to the extent that it existed has traditionally fallen on the shoulders of the individual teachers. In such a scenario, it is improbable that external demands will result in people's shaping up. Elmore captures this beautifully:

> It seems unlikely to us that schools operating in the default mode—where all questions of accountability related to student learning are essentially questions of individual teacher responsibility—will be capable of responding to strong obtrusive accountability systems in ways that lead to systematic deliberate improvement of instruction and student learning. The idea that a school will *improve,* and therefore, [so will] the overall performance of its students implies a capacity for collective deliberation and action that schools in our sample did not exhibit. Where virtually all decisions about accountability are made by individual teachers, based on their individual conceptions of what they and their students can do, it seems unlikely that these decisions will somehow aggregate into overall improvement for the school. (2004, p. 197)

Addressing atomistic cultures with external interventions that cannot work takes us back to that sad personal feeling of "If I am in a bad relationship, I'd rather be alone." Collaborative school and district cultures—still a minority, but there are more and more—find typical current accountability systems to be simply clunky distractions. Current external accountability systems in education are designed, ineptly as it turns out, to hunt down the bottom performers by loading on tests and demanding action, while slowing down those cultures that are on the move.

In my book *The Principal,* I document how well-meant micromanagement requirements have brought schools to a standstill. Here is one of many examples from two of the leading practitioners (former highly effective principals and superintendents) Rick DuFour and Mike Mattos (2013), who comment on the new accountability policies in the state of Tennessee:

> Principals or evaluators must observe new teachers six times each year and licensed teachers four times each year, considering one or more of four areas—instruction, professionalism, classroom environment, and planning. These four areas are further divided into 116 subcategories. Observations are to be preceded by a pre-conference, in which the principal and the teacher discuss the lesson, and followed by a post-conference, in which the principal shares his or her impressions of the teacher's performance. Principals must then input data on the observation using the state rubric for assessing teachers. Principals report that the process requires four to six hours for each observation. (Fullan, 2013, p. 43)

How many hours are there in the day? Imagine raising your children that way! We saw in the previous chapter that without the value of autonomy and cooperative group work, managers are stuck with having to add ever more complicated procedures designed to monitor performance. The end result is that almost no one is happy, including individual teachers who want things to improve, as they see some colleagues, and officials higher up in the system, acting in less than responsible ways. With an accountability system that causes *less* rather than more responsibility, it is no wonder that most teachers want to see external accountability go away.

But that would be only the "freedom from" outcome. What would the "freedom to" solution look like, and how can individuals and those around them bring it about? This is the new, more powerful internal accountability that could back up a repositioned external accountability that I'll describe later on.

Internal Accountability: A More Cultural Approach

Internal accountability, which I will spell out in this section, is based on the notion that individuals *and* the group in which they work can transparently hold themselves responsible for their performance. We already know that current external accountability schemes do not work because, at best, they tell us that the system is not performing (they notice poor results) but do not give a clue about *how* to fix the situation. As Elmore (2004) observes, if people do not know how to fix the problem and therefore cannot do so, "schools will implement the requirements of the external accountability system in pro forma ways without ever internalizing the values of responsibility and efficacy that are the nominal objectives of those systems" (p. 134). Elmore then concludes that "investments in internal accountability *must logically precede* any expectation that schools will respond productively to external pressure for performance" (p. 134, italics added).

"Logically precede," yes; but more to the point of this discussion, *strategically* precede, in a process of cultural shift. There are two messages here. One is that policymakers and other leaders are well advised to establish conditions for developing cultures of internal accountability. The second is that there are things other people can do when the hierarchy is not inclined to move. The answer is to help make it happen in your own situation—in other words, develop collaborative work with your peers and push upward for this work to be supported.

What is the so-called cultural approach? As we have seen, the history of the teaching profession is laced with assumptions of and conditions for atomistic, individual responsibility. But atomistic responsibility, detached from any group, can never work. In a nutshell, the cultural shift needed is toward the development of collaborative cultures that honor and align individual responsibility with collective expectations and actions. With this kind of cultural cohesion—promoting autonomy *and* cooperation—the individual and the group are equally valued.

Elmore (2004) discusses several schools that he and his team studied. Most of them exemplify the individualistic model. Teachers work away on their own and periodically grapple or clash with external accountability requirements. But Elmore also discusses two cases where the schools have developed more or less collaborative cultures. At St. Aloysius elementary school, for example,

> Without exception, teachers described an atmosphere of high expectations. Some stressed a high priority on "reaching every child" and "making sure that no one is left behind" while others referred to a serious and supportive

environment where everyone is expected to put forth excellent work. (p. 164)

Sounds ideal, but what happens when things don't go as expected? At another school, Turtle Haven, Elmore asked teachers, "What happens when teachers do not meet the collective expectations?" He reports that most teachers believed that a person who did not "meet expectations, or conform to a culture created by those expectations would first receive a great deal of support from the principal and other colleagues" (2004, p. 183).

If this approach failed to produce results, most Turtle Haven teachers said that the teacher in question would not be happy at the school and eventually would either

> "weed themselves out" [or] eventually, if there was a sense in the community that a certain number of children were not able to get the kind of education that we say we're committed to providing, we would have to think whether the somebody belongs here or not. (Elmore, 2004, p. 183)

This kind of culture is not foolproof, but I would say that it stacks up well against the external accountability thinking that creates demands that go unheeded or can't be acted on. In collaborative cultures, the internal accountability system is based on visible expectations combined with consequences for failure to meet those expectations.

Such cultures, says Elmore, are much better equipped to deal with external accountability requirements, adding that a school with a strong internal accountability culture might respond to an external assessment system in a number of ways "including accepting and internalizing it; rejecting it and developing defenses against it, or incorporating just those elements of the system that the school or the individuals deem relevant" (2004, p. 145).

What is coming through in this discussion is that collaborative cultures with an eye to continuous improvement establish internal processes that allow them to sort out differences and make effective decisions.

I encountered an interesting version of this phenomenon in Australia. My colleagues and I were working as consultants to the Australian Capital Territories. One of the high schools had introduced a coaching feedback model; they had trained two people in the use of a "quality teaching framework" to give teachers feedback on their teaching. We found that many teachers were doubtful about the procedure or outright against it ("I don't want someone coming into my classroom telling me what to do"). Three years later when we returned to do some filming in this particular school, we found that all teachers were engaged in the coaching-feedback process, and touting it as responsible for improvements in their teaching. What had happened?

I asked the following question of the deputy principal: "When we were here three years ago, many teachers were against the coaching model, and now everyone is embracing it. Is the practice voluntary or inevitable?" Without hesitation he responded, "It is voluntary but inevitable." Now that's a good change process! What they had done was to introduce the coaching practice with a clear agreement that they expected everyone to participate, but that it was up to the participants to decide whether or not to act on the feedback (shades of Pixar's candor *and* autonomy). Also, they had refined the process based on feedback from teachers.

Push Me, Pull Me

The Australian example encompasses elements of feedback and internal accountability, as the leadership and the group acted to improve teaching across the school. It also captures what we have learned about an effective change process, namely that it shapes and reshapes good ideas as it builds capacity and ownership. Both the good idea and the good process are what count: the *pull* of the good idea and the *push* (with increasing pull as the idea becomes more attractive) supplied by the process. Such a process reflects indirect accountability built into the culture of interaction.

Andy Hargreaves and I have identified both "pull" and "push" as powerful and necessary factors to combine for success (Hargreaves & Fullan, 2012). *Pull* refers to the way that people are attracted to a compelling vision and to working with colleagues and leaders who are talented and committed to working together toward a compelling destination. *Push* refers to climates in which expectations are high and explicit, and peers interact working on common goals; there is push when practice and results are transparent and when regular discussions occur about what is and is not working. Such cultures continually press for (push for) improvement.

What is sometimes missed is how "pushy"' collaborative cultures are about moving the organization and the people in it forward. Hargreaves, Boyle, and Harris (2014) have found "pushy pressure" in the very high performing organizations they studied: "Uplifting leadership harnesses the power of the group to push and pull the team to complete their challenging journey together" (p. 12). Uplifting leadership "combines the pull of strong allegiances with powerful peer pressure" (p. 94).

The fellowship of the team devoted to an inspiring purpose is what lets team members push and pull one another forward (recall Joe Rantz and the Olympic rowers in *Boys in the Boat*). Peers can deploy way more pressure than any hierarchy can muster. That is because they strike a balance of high expectations and empathy. These cultures generate strong allegiance to the cause *and to each other.* If people are not performing, they are helped, not berated. Pretty soon the organization consists of people who are good at getting the best out of each other. Talent attracts talent. Good people working with other good people get even better. Talented organizations improve weak members. When they don't see change in progress, talented individuals leave weak organizations. The net result is ever-increasing collective efficacy.

Another feature of these cultures of internal accountability is that they have a high degree of *precision and transparency.* One of the great problems of learning anything concerns how to grasp the clarity and specificity of the new idea or practice. I suspect that many people fail to learn things not because they are against the idea but because they simply don't get it. The most powerful thing about working with others daily is that you do have a strong chance of learning something. The depth of knowledge becomes greater and especially *the shared depth of understanding* of what you are doing with the group.

If these push-and-pull cultures do not seem strong enough, ask yourself the question, "Compared to what?" These collective cultures with high expectations, transparent practices, and corrective actions *are incredibly strong.* Since 2003, I have served as education policy adviser to the government in Ontario, where we have built such a culture across the public school system, with strategic investment in collaborative, responsive cultures and limited overt punitive accountability. The results speak for themselves: a substantial increase in high school graduation rates (from 68 percent to 83 percent in the nine hundred schools), large increases in literacy, and a major reduction in the gap between high- and low-performing schools. We are not talking about individual schools, but rather the whole system— entire districts and the system itself, with two million students and over one hundred thousand teachers (see Fullan & Rincon-Gallardo, in press, for a full account of the Ontario story).

Some Running Conclusions

Let's see what our select dozen had to say about accountability (and, to note again, I selected them as educators who are highly successful—that is, they employ collaborative cultural solutions to performance):

> Accountability [in our situation] is now primarily described as an accountability for student learning. It is less about some test result and more about accepting ownership of the moral imperative of having every student learn. Teachers talk about "monitoring" differently. As they engage in greater sharing of the work, they talk about being accountable, as people in the school community know what they are doing, and looking to see what is changing for students as a result. And as they continue to deprivatize teaching, they talk about their principal and peers coming into their classrooms and expecting to see

the work [of agreed-on practices] reflected in their teaching, their classroom walls, and student work.

—Government official

Teachers and administrators talk about accountability by deprivatizing their practice. If everyone knows what the other teacher or administrator is working on and how they are working on it with students, it becomes a lot easier to talk about accountability. When everyone has an understanding of accountability, creating clear goals and steps to reach those goals, it makes it easier for everyone to talk and work in accountable environments.

—Elementary principal

I spoke with my staff about accountability versus responsibility in brainstorming about what is our purpose and who is responsible for what, as we became more explicit . . .

—Secondary school principal

We are moving to define accountability as responsibility. My district has been engaged in some important work that speaks to intrinsic motivation, efficacy, perseverance, etc., and accountability is seen as doing what is best for students . . . working together to tackle any challenge, and being motivated by our commitment as opposed to some external direction.

—Superintendent

When you blow down the doors and walls, you can't help but be ever more accountable.

—Superintendent

I do believe that a lot of work remains to be done on building common understanding on the notion of accountability.
Many people still believe that someone above them in the hierarchy is accountable. Very few take personal accountability for
student learning and achievement. There are still those who
blame parents and student's background for achievement.

—Consultant

In one school the talk about accountability was pervasive
as the school became designated as underperforming. The
morale of the school went down significantly, and the tension was omnipresent at every meeting. The team switched
the conversation to motivation, innovation, and teamwork,
and the culture changed. The school is energized, and the test
scores went up in one year. The team is now committed to
results and continuous improvement.

—Consultant

Let's gather up some conclusions that we have reached so far
about the cultural approach to accountability.

First, look back at the second-to-last comment, which
says that too many individual teachers do not internalize
personal responsibility (that is, accountability) for ensuring
that all students in their classrooms achieve. Point taken. My
response in this section is that the best route to creating a
more responsible culture is to focus on the collective expectations and transparent performance of teachers, in effect
mobilizing support and built-in pressure for taking responsibility for student learning.

Second, the last quotation notes that negative external
pressure triggered action. Again, point well taken. We can

acknowledge the value of negative external accountability, provided that the response switches to the collaborative strategy as a solution. What is happening in these cases is that policymakers are trying with obtrusive external accountability to do at the back end what they should have done at the front end (years ago) by investing in internal accountability. (For a related brilliant argument and explanation of how the teaching profession in the United States evolved, see *The Allure of Order*, by Harvard professor Jal Mehta, 2013.) Back-loaded accountability at best stops the bleeding in dying schools. If you want a deeper and sustainable accountability, it has to be *culturally based*.

Third, I believe I've made the case with lots of negative evidence (about how current negative accountability doesn't work) and with positive evidence (how internal cultures of accountability do) that the solution lies in the development of cultures in which individuals and groups continuously acquire greater shared depth of understanding about the nature of the work and its performance (Fullan, 2011).

Fourth, we've seen how these internal cultures foster a pull-and-push peer culture with leaders who help create the conditions that press accountability forward.

Fifth, we've seen that these cultures can and do engage the external accountability system; they proactively use the external system while also becoming more effective in dealing with it. In Ontario, as noted, we have built up internal accountability through collaborative cultures, combined with transparency of performance, both internal and external to the school. Such schools take into account external assessments of student performance, including using them as a stimulus for further action.

Sixth, a perverse element of neglecting internal accountability is that the organization has to employ increasingly counterproductive negative accountability to address the growing problems of low performance. As more and more employees are disengaged, and as capacity fails to develop, the organization is forced to fall back on carrot-and-stick forms of accountability. It gets stuck in minimal performance that takes more and more energy to maintain, which in turn results in layering on more and more complicated procedures. Strengthening external accountability is a mug's game, not a solution.

By contrast, internal accountability is good for just about everyone. It meets all the requirements I have been laying out in this book: respect for autonomy, connection to others, and feedback about progress. The bottom line is that it produces forceful accountability in a way that no hierarchy can possibly match. I have shown this to be the case for teachers, and if I had more space, I could map out the parallel argument for students. If we want students to be more accountable, we need to change instruction toward employing methods that increase individual students' responsibility for assessing their own learning, and we need to increase peer accountability as students work in groups to assess and provide feedback to one another under the guidance of the teacher. This is exactly what we are doing in our New Pedagogies for Deep Learning initiative (newpedagogies.org), mentioned in chapter 4, with one thousand schools around the world.

Seventh and finally, we always need to loop our efforts at creating internal accountability back to autonomy, cooperation, and feedback. The cultural solution, though subject to cautions about groupthink, makes the group and the individuals within it stronger. You've seen also that feedback is a prized feature of these cultures. They thrive on constant, purposeful day-to-day interaction about the work.

Back to External Accountability

Now let's go back to external accountability and how it can be improved. External accountability concerns any entity that has authority over you. Its presence is still essential, but we need to reposition external accountability so that it becomes more influential in the performance of individuals, groups, and the system as a whole.

The first thing to note is that if the external body invests in building widespread internal accountability, that body will be furthering its own goals of greater organizational or system accountability. The more that internal accountability thrives, the greater the responsiveness to external requirements, and the less the external body has to do—there's less need to resort to carrots and sticks to incite the system to act responsibly.

Dislodging top-down accountability from its increasingly miscast role has turned out to be exceeding difficult. People at the top do not like to give up control. They cling to it despite obvious evidence that it does not work. And attacks on the inadequacy of top-down accountability have failed because they have only focused on the "from" side of freedom. Critics seem to be saying that accountability requirements do not work, so they should be removed. That is not the solution— it takes us back to nothing. The answer needs to be found in determining what kind of external accountability is needed in order to advance the "freedom to" solution. If you reduce constraints, what fills the vacuum?

Central authorities should focus their efforts on two interrelated activities:

1. Investing in internal accountability.

2. Projecting and protecting the system. (Projecting is setting clear goals; protecting is taking action when performance is persistently low.)

By the first I mean investing in the conditions that cause internal accountability to get stronger. The beauty of this approach, as we have seen, is that people throughout the system start doing the work of accountability. Although indirect, this form of accountability is really more explicit, more present, and of course more effective. I have already suggested its components:

- A small number of ambitious goals, and processes that foster shared goals (and even targets if jointly shaped)

- Good data that are used primarily for developmental purposes

- Implementation strategies that are transparent, whereby people and organizations are grouped to learn from each other (using the group to change the group)

- Examination of progress in order to problem-solve for greater performance

Central authorities need to invest in these very conditions that result in greater focus, capacity, and commitment *at the level of day-to-day practice.* They invest, in other words, in establishing conditions for greater local responsibility. In this process, the center will still want goals, standards, assessment, proof of implementation, and evidence of progress. But in order to get results they must invest in resources and mechanisms of internal accountability that people can use to collaborate within their units and across them.

Morieux and Tollman (2014, pp. 131–132) show how an organization increased its performance by "creating networks of interaction" around specific strategies that in effect increased accountability on the spot. One network they describe got together periodically for each person to present his or her latest buying strategy. Another set of groups met to compare the productivity of their teams. In these situations, people gained new ideas but also risked loss of reputation with peers. People also helped each other, which I mention by way of highlighting the accountability component of the networks. Morieux and Tollman note, "Risk-taking is a good thing only when there is cooperation . . . People take risks when they know they can count on the cooperation of others—to compensate, relay, absorb, or provide a safety net in case things go wrong" (p. 170). The idea is to develop the group and individuals in concert. You can see how this relates to building human and social capital. Cooperative cultures raise the capacity of nearly all individuals, and enable the best to become even better and more helpful to others.

In addition to investing in collaborative learning cultures, external bodies can also reinforce the enterprise with policies that establish standards for employees and leaders and that carry over into job descriptions for hiring and developing people. These formal policies reinforce the direction, but by themselves can never carry the day. In that regard, I am reminded of one of the findings from Harvard professor Susan Moore Johnson (2004) in her book *Finders and Keepers: Helping New Teachers Thrive and Survive in Our Schools.*

She examined the effect of mentoring on new teachers, and discovered that beginning teachers who received one-to-one mentoring in schools that had individualistic cultures, compared to teachers who received such mentoring in collaborative cultures, were more likely to struggle and drop out of the profession. Even though the policy was similar (one-to-one help), collaborative cultures had the hidden benefit of more helpful colleagues. These schools were evidently better places to work and develop. In short, central authorities can greatly enhance accountability by directly investing in the conditions that maximize collaboration in the culture.

Because this book focuses mainly on individuals and groups in terms of what they can do to enjoy "freedom to" opportunities, I won't spell out more of how system leaders might invest in fostering transparent collaborative cultures. I'll move on briefly to how they can best project and protect a highly collaborative system. In essence, they can establish goals and expectations, set standards, be transparent about progress, and intervene selectively in cases of persistent failure. It helps to publicly, on a regular basis, highlight the aspiration of the system, publish results about progress toward the goals, and be willing to intervene to address weakness of performance. Constant transparency is not a bad accountability weapon in its own right. Beyond that, there should be intervention strategies.

It is best at the outset to commit first to turnaround policies that are based on capacity-building intervention and support. Our turnaround strategy for Ontario's low-performing or stuck schools (called the Ontario Focused Intervention Partnership) is quite explicit. Student achievement data identify the problems; capacity-building training is direct; teachers and schools are linked to other schools similar in demographics to learn about practices that work. At the beginning in 2004, more than eight hundred of the four thousand elementary schools fell into this lower performance grouping. Today only sixty-nine schools are there.

A large part of the problem with low-performing units is not resistance but lack of capacity. Once you take this developmental approach, a large percentage of the problem (but not all) is addressed without rancor. People love to improve, especially if they have had little success. Successful turnaround unleashes new energy for those involved and others connected to them.

Protecting Your Own Interests and Those of the Group

The system must protect itself, and so must you. However, living successfully in the "freedom to" world is a little more complex than just looking after number one. In the "freedom to" world, you need also to connect with others, especially peers. Recall Fromm's advice that the solution will be found in our relationships with others: humans are primarily social beings. The Pulitzer Prize winner Tina Rosenberg (2011) makes this point forcefully in *Join the Club: How Peer Pressure Can Transform the World.* Tough problems, she argues (and demonstrates with case examples), require a *social cure* within which the most powerful incentive is "helping people obtain what they most care about: respect of their peers" (p. xix). We saw this earlier as well, that one of the top two or three motivators for humans is camaraderie with peers engaged in doing something worthwhile. Let's consider the implications of this orientation from three perspectives: your own, that of your peers, and that of people above you.

This book should convince you that even in the most selfish sense, you are fundamentally better off when you connect to others around you. Take the terrible case with which we started the chapter: the novice teacher thrown into a low-accountability school. If she is to have any hope of surviving, she must reach out to one or more peers for help. This is a brave act in a seemingly unsupportive culture, but it is where "freedom to" lies. We have to create our own accountability (responsibility) by making a connection to potential helpers.

Not only the novice but even the most seemingly self-sufficient person is better off connecting. If you want to improve yourself or want to make a bigger difference with those around, above, and below you, the single most powerful thing you can do is to join with peers. Rosenberg makes the same point. She argues that the typical approaches of giving people more information or attempting to motivate them through fear do not work: "These strategies tend to fail exactly when the issue becomes most salient and emotionally fraught" (2011, p. xix). This point is crucial because all change typically is accompanied by anxiety, fear, and ambiguity—another reason to have supportive peers.

Rosenberg tells us that in essence, "identification with others" in pursuit of an important goal motivates people much more than information or abstract visions. You could take this from the perspective of the leader, as my colleagues and I have in much of our work—if you want to change the group, use the group to change the group—but here I take the individual's point of view. If you, personally, want to grow and do something of importance to you, cultivate your connection with peers who want to move in the same direction. If you want to influence peers (to make the overall culture better or to deal with an annoying peer or boss), again, join in the cause. Rosenberg found that what was most motivating for people in these cases were "genuine friendships, shared experience of helping others, and personal accountability" (2011, p. 171)—this latter being a sense of responsibility to correct or otherwise improve something, with the aid of internal accountabilities.

In the midst of these suggestions, I repeat the underlying caveat about groupthink. As I said in chapter 3, peers are powerful, which means they can be powerfully right or powerfully wrong. Peer pressure can cause us to go along with the group when it is doing something wrong, and even to join in. This is why autonomy is part of the "freedom to" package—have your own moral compass, get away from the group now and then, enjoy reflective solitude. Being both apart from and part of the group is a tension worth having.

Lastly, and one could say politically, you'll want to develop peer power so that you can be more influential upward—either to become better partners with those above you (if they are willing or can be made to see the value in it) or to contend more effectively with unwanted impositions. Even here there are bigger fish to fry. The end game is not to thwart a specific policy or to get rid of a specific odious leader but rather to change the culture of the system that lies behind the bad policy or bad leader. For this you need the group.

Take Action

Ask yourself these questions:

☐ By what standards do my peers and I judge ourselves? How transparent are we about what we are doing and what we feel accountable for?

☐ When I discuss accountability with others, do I always also talk about my own responsibility? Should I?

☐ How often and how well do I and my peers (or members of a group I lead or teach) communicate with each other about our own and our collective responsibilities?

☐ Am I being held accountable for something I don't believe I control? With whom could I talk about that?

☐ When do I fall into groupthink?

☐ What can I do to increase my sense of responsibility relative to key goals, even if the system is not helping?

☐ How can I connect with peers to increase collective responsibility and efficacy with respect to our priorities?

Next

In chapter 6, we widen the group lens to take up the theme of how to be more influential in the larger system, and how to benefit from it. One of the most powerful strategies that we have employed recently for addressing the complexity of system change is called "leadership from the middle" (Hargreaves & Braun, 2012). Beyond this, we will examine the fascinating area of how ideas diffuse in an organization or system.

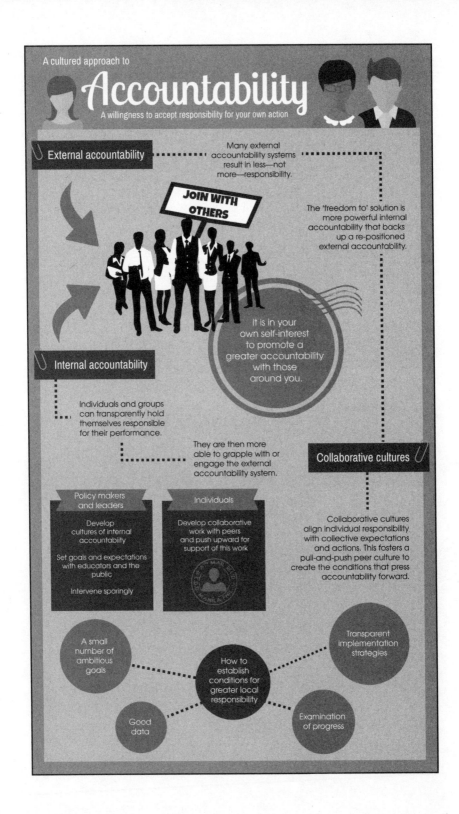

A cultured approach to

Accountability

A willingness to accept responsibility for your own action

External accountability

Many external accountability systems result in less—not more—responsibility.

JOIN WITH OTHERS

The 'freedom to' solution is more powerful internal accountability that backs up a re-positioned external accountability.

It is in your own self-interest to promote a greater accountability with those around you.

Internal accountability

Individuals and groups can transparently hold themselves responsible for their performance.

They are then more able to grapple with or engage the external accountability system.

Collaborative cultures

Collaborative cultures align individual responsibility with collective expectations and actions. This fosters a pull-and-push peer culture to create the conditions that press accountability forward.

Policy makers and leaders

Develop cultures of internal accountability

Set goals and expectations with educators and the public

Intervene sparingly

Individuals

Develop collaborative work with peers and push upward for support of this work

A small number of ambitious goals

Good data

How to establish conditions for greater local responsibility

Transparent implementation strategies

Examination of progress

CHAPTER · SIX

Diffusion

You shouldn't have to be responsible for saving the world, but you probably sense that in a way, you are. Rosenberg (2011) cites a survey of young people in which they list their most important job requirements: "work that helps others, allows them to impact their world, surrounds them with idealistic and committed coworkers, and requires creativity" (p. 182). In our work with schools engaged in "new pedagogies for deep learning," the new learning focuses on real-life problems as the curriculum, and the deep learning consists of six Cs: character education (resilience, perseverance, reliability); citizenship (global knowledge, respect for other cultures); collaboration; communication; creativity; and critical thinking. One school names the bottom line as producing "global critical thinkers collaborating to save the world." For the schools we are working with, these are not just slogans. The schools are making these aspirations part and parcel of daily learning that now goes much beyond the nine-to-three school day.

When organizational people talk about proliferating change, they generally begin from one of two models: scaling or diffusion. For several reasons here, I much prefer diffusion, as I'll explain. Diffusion dovetails well with another concept that is useful for thinking about individual and group change, rather than the top-down kind. That concept is "leadership from the middle," and we'll get into that, too. I'll expand on the implications by looking mainly at three large school systems where diffusion of the collaborative accountability style is making or could make a great difference. Alongside the notion of diffusion is the idea of social networks. The implication of this chapter is that system leaders should invest in networks and collaboratives of learning, and that individuals should seek learning networks even if the system is not cultivating them.

A theme of this chapter is what my colleagues and I call *systemness*. Systemness is one's awareness and commitment to contributing to the larger system, and to benefit from it. For example, when a school moves from being an individualistic culture to a collaborative one, the following thing happens every time: individual teachers stop thinking only of "my kids" in "my classroom" and start thinking of "our kids" in the whole school. This is an increment of systemness, thinking and acting in ways that benefit (even if slightly in this case) the larger system, and you in turn benefit when others also contribute to the same system. Ultimately, global sustainability involves identifying with and doing something that helps improve the bigger picture (see Fullan & Quinn, 2015, and Hargreaves & Shirley, 2012). For these schools the new motto seems to be: developing great citizens for tomorrow, by becoming great citizens today.

Even though I will talk about how systems and system leaders can create the conditions for more action from peers within the system, remember that you as an individual need not and should not wait for them. Be proactive, up and out, to realize your autonomy-cooperation, feedback, and accountability potential.

Diffusion Rather Than Scaling

Hierarchical models, even the best of them, tend to define the problem of enlarging good ideas and practices as "how to get to scale" with them. Scaling is based on the assumption that effective change best occurs when you develop a good idea or program and then try to spread or scale it up to others who could benefit from it. This seems reasonable, and for some purposes scaling can be a useful approach, but for our purposes it fits less well because the focus is on the program. *Diffusion* is a better term because it connotes the spread of good ideas that are adapted as people take them on, or the seeking and adaptation of ideas from others. Scaling and diffusion are overlapping terms, but I want to place greater emphasis on the individual and group. The concept of diffusion takes me back again to my early sociology days as a graduate student. The father of Diffusion of Innovations was Everett Rogers, who has since published the fifth edition of his basic textbook on diffusion (2003). The origin of the study of diffusion began in the 1930s in rural Iowa, as researchers tried to figure out how innovations in farming practices (for example, use of hybrid seeds that increased production) spread to farmers across the state and beyond. Diffusion studies proliferated over the globe, looking at a wide range of practices—for example, how new medical practices and medications were taken up, the boiling of water in Peruvian villages, and the adoption of snowmobiles in the Arctic.

Rogers defines diffusion as "the process in which an innovation is communicated through certain channels over time among the members of a social network" (2003, p. 5). He goes on to say, "The heart of the diffusion process consists of interpersonal network exchanges and social modeling by individuals who are influenced to follow their lead" (p. 35). If we left the definition there, you can see the problem: diffusion favors the well connected, thereby increasing the gap between the haves and the have-nots, and is amenable to manipulation as advocates promote products that are self-serving.

But we won't leave diffusion in its old form. The new diffusion model integrates the best of hierarchical and lateral thinking. In the next section, I will show how the natural limitations of hierarchical systems are yielding to new and more effective adaptations that are more akin to the diffusion model. All of this is compatible with Pentland's social physics paradigm (2014) that I discussed in chapter 3. Recall that he found that individuals learn best by interacting with others to discover new ideas and solve problems. Pentland makes an important distinction between *engagement* and *exploration,* saying that we need both:

> Engagement is social learning, usually within a peer group, that typically leads to the development of behavioral norms and social pressures to enforce those norms. In companies, work groups with a high rate of idea flow among the members of the work group tend to be more productive.
>
> Exploration is the process of searching out new potentially valuable ideas by building and mining diverse social networks. In companies, work groups that have a high rate of idea flow from outside the work group tend to be more innovative. (2014, pp. 19–20)

Leadership from the Middle

Compatible with diffusion thinking, the concept of *leadership from the middle* (LftM) arose from two conclusions our team reached in our work exploring and enabling change: (1) in large systems, top-down change doesn't work because you can't directly control large systems from the top; (2) hierarchical systems press to engage the entire system in change—all components or as close to all as possible. But even well-run hierarchies can only do so much. By "well-run" I mean that they have good leadership at the top, they have focused goals, and they invest in capacity building, develop, monitor, and intervene. They get results, *but there is a limit.* With a hierarchical strategy, you cannot possibly create the kind of "freedom to" conditions that would free up and engage the energies of vast swathes of the system. Similarly, bottom-up change fails in that it produces only ad hoc pockets of change that do not connect and are unlikely to last over time. The question then becomes *Where is the coherence—where is the "glue"?* We find it "in the middle."

The middle can be defined variously depending on what system or part thereof you refer to. Consider education. In statewide systems, the middle comprises the school districts. (The top is the state, and the bottom is local schools.) Within a district, schools are the middle, sandwiched by the district on top and classrooms below. For schools, the middle is individual teachers sandwiched between the school and the students. And so on. Wherever you are, you are part of some middle. The idea is that you work with peers to strengthen the middle, get more things done, and become better partners (or forces for change) upward and downward. In the context of this book, you want to play out your autonomy-cooperation, feedback, and accountability by making a contribution to strengthening from your own middle spot.

Your middle is where you find yourself and your group. From there, you can use Pentland's findings from the group perspective (How do we improve the performance of the company and my role in it?) or from the individual point of view (How can I increase idea flow for my own growth?). Actually, you can use both, embracing the usual tension between yourself and a group. One can get too absorbed by a group. Do you want to risk losing your autonomy, or do you want to stay isolated and risk losing your sanity? It is a productive tension—something to manage rather than to avoid or ignore.

As an inspiration for policy, the concept of LftM implies increasing the role of the middle level as an agent of cohesion and progress. Although LftM is still a new concept, we have found already that it is instantly embraced by school people, who have suffered long over the years from the back-and-forth swing from top-down to bottom-up solutions. (If you have been in this business long enough, you can get hit by the same pendulum more than once.) You don't have to use LftM lingo as long as you grasp the concept. If you can mobilize the middle, you get greater system cohesion and conditions for better coordination upward and downward. From your perspective as an individual, you can participate proactively within the middle (however small your chunk of it might be) in order to gain from the knowledge and the relationships and to help others so gain. Again, you can think of this in terms of a larger good—being part of a broader change. You can also think of it selfishly, so to speak: I fulfill my own goals and myself by working on a strong moral purpose, motivated further by teaming up with others. Both of these are intrinsic motivations for humans.

The key idea is this: *become a better partner upward and downward*. Being in the middle puts you in the best position to improve things by integrating vertical and horizontal forces. You'll do better because you are part of improving something that is worthwhile. And although leveraging the middle for greater change is bigger than you as an individual, it is not remote because you are personally contributing. The middle is big, but not too big.

The implications of all this apply to everyone in the system. Let's start within the school. If you are a teacher—in the middle—you should want to interact with peers to improve the situation. All the better if you have school leaders who want to help make this happen; all the more important if you have a less than effective school leader. If you are a school leader, you have a double assignment: help teachers work together, and link to other schools for mutual learning and development. Thus a diffusion strategy with specificity—LftM—emerges.

I said earlier that educators "instantly embrace" LftM. It is one of those "sticky" concepts that is immediately attractive to people in organizations. Whether they have been beavering away in good hierarchical systems, suffering from top-down imposition, or drifting away in decentralized seas of confusion, people see LftM as something that they can own. It's true that leaders in the middle (superintendents, principals, and bossy peer teachers) can be just as authoritarian as individuals at the top, but any potential for productive liberation is perceived much more readily when diffusion rather than scaling is the point of departure. I should also say that the LftM strategy is in its early stages, so the best models are still being developed and tested. They must pass the specificity test of relevance, rigor, and performance. For example, simply establishing networks and exchange of information not linked to action is *not* what I mean by LftM. These new solutions have to have their proof points so that the participants and others can learn from them. The good news is that frustrated educators—the vast majority—are instantly attracted to the possibility of this approach because they can readily see their role in the process.

Santiago Rincon-Garrardo and I (2015) have recently applied LfMt thinking in order to guide the rapidly (and messily) emerging field of networks, collaboratives, clusters, and so on. Neither control from the top nor an anything goes laissez-faire approach will work. Based on early evidence, we have identified factors associated with effective collaboration that we are applying to our work in California (see below), and New Zealand where the "system" is attempting to coordinate the work of its 2,500 schools that have been individually autonomous (no school districts) since a policy that was passed in 1989 called "Tomorrow's Schools." We have formulated eight guidelines (quite compatible of course with "freedom to change"): develop high trust relationships; focus on ambitious goals; improve instructional practice; deliberate leadership; frequent interaction; connect outwards; build partnerships with students, teachers, and families; and secure adequate resources. This set of factors, if you like, represents a purposeful diffusion model.

A few large school systems and districts are already making strides through fostering LftM. Three examples I will present in the next sections deal with Ontario, Singapore, and California. The first two are successful systems that are shifting their strategies to what is in effect the "freedom to" domain—establishing structures and strategies designed to free up the ideas within the system while harnessing the best ones for the benefit of all. California is in catch-up mode with exciting possibilities.

Ontario's Diffusion and LftM

Ontario began its deliberate foray into whole-system success in 2003 when a provincial election brought in the Liberal party, led by Premier Dalton McGuinty. Ontario embraces thirteen million people, almost 5,000 schools (4,000 elementary and 900 secondary), with two million students and over one hundred thousand educators organized in seventy-two local school districts. In 2003, the performance of the public education system had been flat for the previous five years with respect to literacy, numeracy, and high school graduation rates. Starting in 2003, we established a relatively centrally driven strategy, along with local supports. By and large, it worked—high school graduation rates climbed from 68 percent to 83 percent, literacy (on a high standard of deep learning) moved from 54 percent to 75 percent. What evolved almost naturally, although it needed to be propelled explicitly, is that we increasingly used what we call "lateral learning among implementers" at various levels of "middle" to get at the best ideas. Within the broad Ontario system, York Region District School Board (YRDSB) exemplifies the evolution that has taken place (Belchetz & Witherow, 2014).

York Region is a large, highly diverse district in Ontario, with 120,000 students, 206 schools, and more than eighty-five hundred teaching staff. From 1999 to the present, York has been a leader in moving the yardsticks of student achievement progressively forward. About halfway through this development, district leaders realized that they could not continue to progress just by orchestrating the agenda from the center. So around 2008, York started to use networks of schools working together to strengthen implementation. This began a transition from exploring not only how to get better at basic literacy and the like but also how to address some of the thornier problems—inquiry-based math, personalized instruction, creativity and well-being, and closing the learning gap completely. There are now twenty-seven networks across the district's four large geographical regions. I should note, however, that York Region's networks have not been evaluated, and they would do well to apply the eight factor framework that Santiago and I developed.

LftM, in this case within the district where the schools are the middle, seeks to operate along the same lines of simplexity that I have identified in this book: melding and integrating autonomy, cooperation, feedback, and accountability. When this is done well—with the sophistication of simplexity and its interaction effects—it unleashes greater local adaptation, ingenuity, ownership, and commitment to go deeper and to sustain learning for individuals and the system alike. What's more, it is contagious. Much as we discussed in chapter 2 in terms of Daniel Pink's work, diffusion strategies like those emerging in York synergize autonomy, mastery, purpose, and cooperation. Good hierarchical systems are effective at continuous improvement but not at engaging in the innovation necessary for deeper solutions. LftM is good at both improvement and innovation. In LftM solutions, the middle becomes more of a force and freer to act, but does so in cooperation with the hierarchical system. Whatever your role in education (if that is your field), I urge you to heed the York lessons. If you are a system leader, develop your version of an LftM strategy. If you are a classroom teacher, connect with some other teachers and the principal to work with peers, and so on.

We also see in Ontario another larger "natural" adoption of the LftM strategy. In the following example, people experienced the value of LftM and wanted to do more. In 2008, Ontario allocated $25 million to CODE (Council of Ontario Directors [that is, superintendents] of Education) to take on the coordination of efforts to implement improvements in special education and overall achievement across the seventy-two districts in the province. This middle layer of districts developed a set of strategies that focused on implementation and on schools and districts learning from each other. Hargreaves and Braun (2012) conducted detailed case studies of ten representative districts (one of which is YRDSB). The research study took place from 2009 to 2011, and showed impressive outcomes in student achievement. In other words, when you give the middle an opportunity and some resources to lead the strategy, it does a very good job (better than the center could have done), and you get deep ownership to boot.

The ten districts got a strong taste of LftM, and liked it so much that they formed a consortium to carry on as a regular way of working. A new proposal issued by the group is called *CODE Consortium for System Leadership and Innovation* (Council of Ontario Directors of Education, 2014). In it, each of the ten districts identifies specific priority projects from which other districts might learn and around which interests and learning can converge. This is autonomy and cooperation at work. A steering group of peers runs the consortium. The group held their first annual symposium in October 2014, to which all the boards of all seventy-two districts in the province were invited. The plan is to open membership to all boards as of

2015–2016. The whole provincial system thus becomes involved in this deepening LftM strategy. But remember that all of this requires partnerships. In this case, these districts will not be successful if they don't extend the same idea to schools within their jurisdictions to be more proactive with peers within and across schools.

Singapore: Tops from the Middle

What about top-performing Singapore? Over the past several years, our team has been in interaction with education leaders at both its national and school levels. Singapore has a small system with some 250 schools; it has been very successful over the past twenty-five years using what I earlier referred to as a very good central model of direction, capacity building, and support. Singapore always performs in the top five countries on the report from the Programme for International Student Assessment (known as PISA, an activity of OECD, the Organization for Economic Cooperation and Development, 2014a), which every three years assesses the achievement of fifteen-year-olds across some sixty-five countries in literacy, math, and science.

Over the past five years, however, Singapore's education leaders, national and local, increasingly sensed that this excellent traditional strategy was not going to work for a future that would require more innovation and adaptability on the ground. So they began to add networks of schools to the mix. All schools are in clusters of up to twenty or more, and focus on common interests. Hargreaves, Boyle, and Harris, who studied

Singapore schools, show that increased cooperation can occur, indeed needs to occur, under Singapore's conditions of competition. At the same time, they observe that schools are committed to show other schools what they have achieved and learned, and to learn from each other. The authors visited Ngee Ann Secondary School, where "the principal Adrian Lim described how the school had opened itself to over sixty-five schools to learn about new technology" (Hargreaves et al., 2014, p. 87). Lim felt that working with another school allowed educators to "really sharpen each other" so that "both schools level up together" (p. 87).

Singaporean educators are also proactive learners about what might be happening around the world. When I recently told a group from the Ministry of Education about our new focus on diffusion versus scaling, they immediately responded that they had better examine the distinction, and instantly (or so it seemed to me) sent me a proposal for research that they are about to launch titled "A System's Model of Scaling: Centralization and Decentralization Balances" (Hung, 2014). They retain the term *scaling*, but wanted to examine how it could include diffusion ideas. The research questions they are about to study include

- What are the characteristics of centralized and decentralized models at play in Singapore schools?
- How do we go about harvesting innovations that can be taken up by the system?
- How do we sustain and encourage diffusion of innovations in schools?

What they are working on is how to integrate vertical and horizontal forces that access innovations and improve all schools in the system. This captures the spirit of LftM, which mobilizes the middle to learn from each other and to be better partners up and down the system.

California—No Longer Just Dreamin'?

What about California—not only *not* a successful education system in recent decades but one where many in the state ruefully say things like, "Yes, we have been a bit of a basket case over the past thirty years"? Our team is working at all levels of the education system in California, where LftM is taking off like wildfire. California is large and complicated to say the least: some forty million people (more than all of Canada); more than seven million students; twenty thousand schools; and 1,009 school districts. California has been one of the lowest-performing U.S. states over the past thirty years.

Observing a failing system, what some people don't appreciate is that there are many individuals who desperately want to succeed, and that pockets of them are getting somewhere against the odds. Given these conditions, combining "freedom from" with "freedom to" strategies could unleash enormous energy and commitment for system change—a scenario ripe for the LftM approach. Several clusters of districts have been formed to focus on deep new improvements and to learn collectively. Fortunately, state leaders Governor Jerry Brown and State Superintendent Tom Torlakson, as well as the State Board of Education, recognize the opportunity and potential and are shifting state resources and policies to support this new way of working. I am optimistic about California's prospects over the next five years because there are so many leaders at all levels who are stepping up to the plate.

Brown has decentralized resources to local districts by radically revamping the funding and accountability requirements (called the Local Control Funding Formula and its corresponding Local Control and Accountability Plan). Districts are clamoring to gather in consortia to work together on common specific solutions. (We ourselves are supporting several of these clusters, and many others are forming, all these districts committing to working together for three or more years at a time.) The statewide Association of California School Administrators is mobilizing to support its members in these endeavors. The State Department of Education is attempting to shift from compliance to capacity building. The California Teachers Association is looking to support the development of the professional capital of its members (although they are sidetracked in combating problematic teacher evaluation schemes). Reconfiguring the role of the fifty-seven county offices that relate to the 1,009 districts is also part of the solution. In addition, several other bodies, such as statewide interest groups including parents' associations, businesses, and scores of foundations, are investing in district consortia. (For an overview of the California education scene, see http://www.michaelfullan.ca/category/california/.)

It is all the better that leaders at different levels of the California system are taking compatible action in the same direction. But these actions will fail if individuals and peers at the local level—students, parents, community leaders, teachers, principals, district leaders—do not proactively take advantage of and push the agenda. Ultimately, it will be individuals and small groups banding together that produce the breakthrough.

California offers a "freedom to" opportunity of colossal proportions.

I am optimistic about California because people at all levels have so readily bought into the strengthening of the LftM strategy in order to bring focus and cohesion to the improvement efforts. California will be the biggest test case we know of that involves jettisoning key distracters (such as dysfunctional funding and constraining tests schemes) in favor of new opportunities (such as strengthening the role and capacity of districts, schools, and communities). Developing the "freedom to" capacity to take advantage of the new possibilities will be the hardest part. As I've noted elsewhere in this book, it is always comparatively easier to get rid of old shackles than it is to take advantage of new freedoms.

The same theme—using the middle to stimulate innovation, ownership, and accountability—is also occurring in business, as we saw earlier. Morieux and Tollman's (2014) "simple rules" four, five, and six serve exactly this purpose. Rule four—increase reciprocity—requires and supports people in the middle to work together in mutually supportive ways. Rule five—extend the shadow of the future—reinforces joint direction by building in feedback loops about progress. Rule six—reward those who cooperate—values transparency, innovation, and ambitious aspirations.

Sutton and Rao (2014), business professors at Stanford University, focus on this same middle domain. Although they happen to use the term *scaling* (*Scaling Up Excellence*), they are clearly addressing mechanisms for purposeful and specific diffusion within the organization. Their book examines "what it takes to build and uncover pockets of exemplary performance [and] spread those splendid deeds" (p. ix). Their stirring phrase "the job of the hierarchy is to defeat the hierarchy," is in the same vein of mobilizing other levels of the organization (p. 107). Sutton and Rao devote a whole chapter to the premise "connect people and cascade excellence" (p. 174). Engaging the middle in collaborative work generates greater cohesion and energy for continuous high performance as the middle connects within itself and across levels.

Will We Take Advantage?

Conditions are becoming gradually more favorable for releasing at least some of the constraints that warrant "freedom from." The challenge will be whether people take advantage of the new opportunities. Success will depend more on whether individuals and groups push for changes than it will on whether system leaders try to make changes happen. The message is to create a win-win scenario where the interests of the individual and the group integrate. But individual and group goals should not completely merge. If they do, we are back to Fromm's authoritarianism. Nor should individual and group goals be divergent, or we will be back to worrisome isolationism.

For leaders, the main lesson is that they should work from the premise that individual and organizational interests are best served by codetermination, by individuals and groups working together and becoming more skilled at balancing the tensions between autonomy and cooperation. Individuals, of course, can still opt out of LftM organizations as much as they did in hierarchical systems, but they are less likely to because the synergy of simplexity draws people in and makes it in their best interest to stay in. Increasingly, individuals will not be better off going it alone. Of course, as I noted before, being in the wrong relationship can be worse than being alone; if individuals find themselves in a bad organization, they should either try to improve it or, if they can, leave. The pressure for creating conditions favorable to the productivity of "freedom to" scenarios should come equally from individuals and the organization.

Back to the Individual

In many ways, we are witnessing the rapid expansion of Pentland's social physics (2014), with its engagement and exploration dynamics. We might call this the "diffusion society," which presents many opportunities to take the initiative on your own and with individuals and groups beside, above, and below you. Social media, networks, and collaboratives are now exploding with opportunities and dangers (waste of time, getting involved with the wrong crowd, becoming overwhelmed with information and options, and so on). Certainly "freedom to" says you must venture into this new world. What I have tried to do in this book is to provide you with a small number of guideposts for the adventure: maintain the balance between autonomy and groupness; seek purposeful feedback relative to your main goals; put yourself in situations of self- and collective responsibility; and, in this chapter, join your middle to leverage better change for yourself and your group.

One thing is for sure. If you remain passive, your future will be determined by other forces. "Freedom from" restraints will limit your options, and "freedom to" choices will be squandered. Venturing out is risky; staying in is stultifying.

Take Action

Ask yourself these questions:

☐ What's the "middle" that I'm part of?

☐ What do I see looking "alongside," "upward," and "downward"?

☐ What changes do I want to see?

☐ What influences do I have in each direction? With whom among those people do I connect well? Is there someone else I could be reaching?

☐ How could I improve on my influence with them in terms of cooperation, feedback, and accountability?

☐ Who needs to hear from me?

☐ What do I need to do, regardless of what the rest are doing? How will I be accountable for that?

Next

I hope chapters 3 through 6 have piqued your interest in, if not equipped you to enter, the "freedom to" world. All that remains is a reminder that you need to find "your own best freedom."

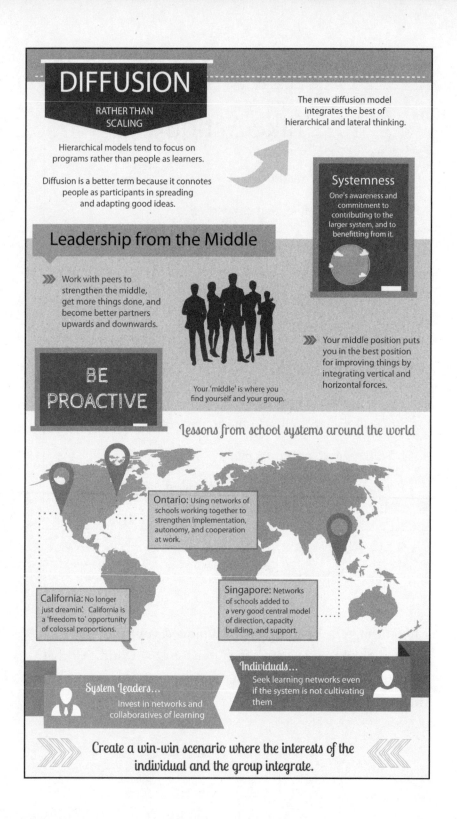

DIFFUSION

RATHER THAN
SCALING

The new diffusion model integrates the best of hierarchical and lateral thinking.

Hierarchical models tend to focus on programs rather than people as learners.

Diffusion is a better term because it connotes people as participants in spreading and adapting good ideas.

Systemness

One's awareness and commitment to contributing to the larger system, and to benefitting from it.

Leadership from the Middle

»» Work with peers to strengthen the middle, get more things done, and become better partners upwards and downwards.

»» Your middle position puts you in the best position for improving things by integrating vertical and horizontal forces.

BE PROACTIVE

Your 'middle' is where you find yourself and your group.

Lessons from school systems around the world

Ontario: Using networks of schools working together to strengthen implementation, autonomy, and cooperation at work.

California: No longer just dreamin'. California is a 'freedom to' opportunity of colossal proportions.

Singapore: Networks of schools added to a very good central model of direction, capacity building, and support.

Individuals…
Seek learning networks even if the system is not cultivating them

System Leaders…
Invest in networks and collaboratives of learning

»» Create a win-win scenario where the interests of the individual and the group integrate. «««

CHAPTER · SEVEN

Your Own Best Freedom

There is no such thing as total freedom—the closer you get to it, the more it disintegrates into nothing or worse. The best me—the freest me—is not being alone to do what I want but rather doing something worthwhile with one or more others. As the young rower Joe Rantz found out, you have to want victory for your teammates, even for those you don't like so well, as much as you want it for yourself. You will also probably find that they become more likeable because most people respond to the way they are treated. And *you* will become more fulfilled in the deal.

What makes us beautifully human is what we do with the tension between being alone and being with others. We need to be good at doing both. Being comfortable in solitary pursuits and teamwork puts us squarely into the world of learning, innovation, and limitless accomplishments. There is no end to this process.

We began this book by understanding the paradox of escape from freedom that Eric Fromm so insightfully laid bare. Constrained humankind loses identity and succumbs to destructive habits. Unencumbered humankind dwells on loneliness and growing anxiety about the meaning and value of life.

Autonomy *and* cooperation in the pursuit of an uplifting purpose are one element of the solution. Another element involves building in feedback loops that create cultures of continuous learning by overcoming the natural tensions involved in feedback between humans. A third relates to "getting accountability right," whereby internal accountability takes the lead, with external accountability playing an "I've got your back" reinforcer and protective role. The fourth is to loosen up hierarchical structures so that they are more amenable to individual and small-group initiative, including leadership from the middle (wherever your middle situates you in the system). Paradoxically, such loosening results in greater cohesion because purposeful interaction is the social glue that binds but does not confine.

Another way of expressing these phenomena is to say that they integrate individual and group dynamics; they similarly mesh vertical and horizontal structures that move systems in the same direction. Horizontal learning—your lateral group—gets at and spreads ideas, and builds capacity and ownership, because there are many more peers than hierarchical leaders. Purposeful peer interaction generates greater cohesion. The value of the hierarchy is in its attending to overall purpose and allocation of resources and its projecting and protecting the system. Horizontal and vertical end up being on the same team.

Take the risk to find your own freedom nested in what I have called connected autonomy. This is a requirement at all times, but might be especially propitious these days. We see more cracks in the old limited freedom scenarios, partly because it is obvious that they don't work (considering that well over half of employees are not engaged in their work, or in their learning when it comes to schools), and partly because finding and pursuing the lines of greater freedom are increasingly essential. Finding new freedoms is crucial in the workplace because the job market is changing radically and has become less predictable. In education, boring education is giving way to exciting new digital learning for all students.

In education, I see new developments expanding rapidly in what we call the "stratosphere" agenda (Fullan, 2013, and www.newpedagogies.org), where thousands of schools are innovating toward engaged learning, and thousands more are moving in this direction.

The movement toward conditions favorable to "freedom to" pursuits is captured also by Warren Berger (2014), the business writer on innovation, entrepreneurialism, and creativity who shows how we need to cultivate the habit of asking "a more beautiful question": "A beautiful question is an ambitious yet actionable question that can begin to shift the way we perceive or think about something—and might serve as a catalyst to bring about change" (p. 8).

The "freedom to" world cries out for more and more beautiful questions: What would I do if I had more freedom? How might I tackle a long-standing problem that has affected my work? What new idea outside the box might I pursue with some of my peers? And so on.

This analysis of "freedom to change" is profoundly compatible with Matthew Crawford's brilliant book, *The World Beyond Your Head: On Becoming an Individual in the Age of Distraction*. Crawford makes the case that society has evolved to the point where, though we operate under the guise of individualism and apparent choice, we are no longer architects of our own lives. Rather than seeking freedom, Crawford argues, we should seek agency—the capacity to act or have some degree of control over complex environments. To achieve something worthwhile we must connect with the environment and with others. Once again, genuine independence can only be achieved by the connected individual.

Henry Mintzberg, a long-standing business professor at McGill, and a bit of a curmudgeon when it comes to organizational and societal ills, has just published a call for radical action by individuals and groups in a book that is right in our "freedom to" wheelhouse. In *Rebalancing Society: Radical Renewal beyond Left, Right, and Center* Mintzberg says that the world has been in a free fall since 1989 where governments and big business are variously exploiting the present at the expense of the future, and are inactive or seemingly powerless to self-correct. Our world, he says, is "dangerously out of balance" (p. 70), with the environment deteriorating in a rapidly linear manner, and social and economic gaps increasing at a phenomenal rate with the top 1 percent accumulating vast amounts of wealth, while all of us seek more and more regardless of the impact on others or our planet. Governments can't fix it; businesses and related corporate entities won't fix it. That leaves, says Mintzberg, "you, me, and we in this troubled world" (p. 69). Taking action to reduce exploitation, whether on a grand scale or with respect to the person down or in the street, will not depend on others but on "you and me," urges Mintzberg.

We are back to the problem that Eric Fromm was grappling with. "Freedom to" will not be resolved by others, nor by working alone. Our freedom lies in constantly addressing our relation to the world, to others, to nature, and to oneself. This could be a moment in time when we are losing our world. Why take a chance? Do good for yourself and others: use the four strategies in this book to put your inner drive into overdrive. Save yourself and the world while you are at it. It won't happen otherwise.

Things still will go wrong. In certain situations, progress or even survival might be impossible. But life would not be life if we got it right easily. Where do you want to put your money and your energy? If you want to be free and want to help others be free, you may be better off working on establishing the synergistic conditions of "freedom to" than fighting the ad hoc obstacles that bind you to the status quo. Even if you win some of the "freedom from" battles, you will be back at square one when it comes to figuring out how to live with your new freedom. For sure, work on overcoming existing constraints, but put more effort into creating the conditions for freedom to do uplifting things that only humans working alone and together can do.

For addressing the complex problem of shifting our minds from unproductive "freedoms from" to productive "freedoms to," simplexity leads us to a wonderfully short set of essentials. As I've said throughout this book, simplexity means getting the right main elements into the mix and cultivating their chemistry. I've summarized them here:

A Simplexity of Greater Freedom

1. Beware of "freedom from"–induced emptiness and isolation.

2. The route to "freedom to" is simplexity: declutter by identifying a small number of powerful factors, and leverage their interactive effects.

3. The foundation of "freedom to" is purpose, camaraderie with peers, mastery, and a degree of autonomy. Autonomy *and* cooperation are a dynamic duo.

4. Feedback is crucial, but difficult to get right because we like autonomy and we like being liked. Place the burden of feedback on the receiver (yourself). Frame your approach

to new freedom as combining an inspiring purpose, seeking and welcoming feedback, quality interaction, transparent data, and candor *and* autonomy. At the end of the day, you decide how proactive you are going to be on addressing this agenda.

5. Turn accountability on its head. Blunt unwanted external accountability, and increase internal (to you and the group) accountability through strengthening responsibility for your and your group's actions and outcomes.

6. Pursue social learning through exploration and engagement. Diffusion, idea flow, and social learning are the fuel you need.

Humankind is in an era of incredible uncertainty. We find ourselves in a miasma of "freedom from" and "freedom to" dynamics. It is crucial that we work on becoming active agents in shaping our futures—individually above all, and then through labyrinths of relationships. You couldn't want for a better challenge—to be truly alive when it matters so much for all of our futures.

The list here is neither long nor beyond our reach. These are all things you can do and help collaborators do as well. Yet they are all it really takes to put yourself on the path of change. You may not be able to escape *from* freedom, but the four keys for learning that I have offered in this book can help you escape *with* freedom. The choice is yours: stay and die in your tracks or fast-track your future using these ideas!

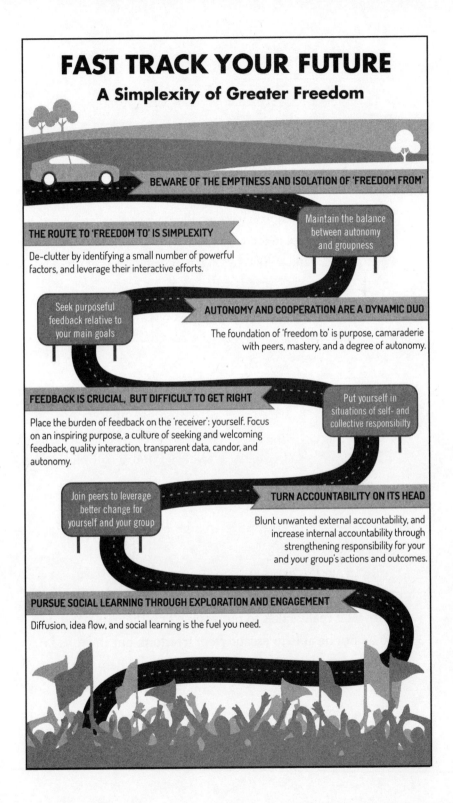

REFERENCES

Asch, S. E. (1951). Effects of group pressure on the modification and distortion of judgments. In H. Guetzkow (Ed.), *Groups, leadership, and men* (pp. 177–190). Pittsburg, PA: Carnegie Press.

Belchetz, D., & Witherow, K. (2014). Ontario district embraces an evolving approach to learning. *Journal of Staff Development, 35*(1), 18–22.

Berger, W. (2014). *A more beautiful question: The power of inquiry to spark breakthrough ideas.* New York, NY: Bloomsbury.

Brown, D. (2014). *Boys in the boat: Nine Americans and their epic quest for gold at the 1936 Berlin Olympics.* New York, NY: Viking.

Catmull, E. (2014). *Creativity, inc.: Overcoming the unseen forces that stand in the way of true inspiration.* New York, NY: Random House.

Council of Ontario Directors of Education. (2014). *CODE Consortium for System Leadership and Innovation.* Toronto: Author.

Crawford, M. (2015). *The world beyond your head: On becoming an individual in the age of distraction.* New York, NY: Farrar, Straus and Giroux.

DuFour, R., & Mattos, M. (2013). How do principals really improve schools? *Education Leadership, 66*(5), 62–68.

Elmore, R. (2004). *School reform from the inside out.* Cambridge, MA: Harvard University Press.

Freedman, L. (2013). *Strategy: A history.* New York, NY: Oxford University Press.

Friedman, R. (2014). *The best place to work.* New York, NY: Penguin Group.

Fromm, E. (1969). *Escape from freedom* (2nd ed.). New York, NY: Holt Paperbacks.

Fullan, M. (2011). *Choosing the wrong drivers for whole system reform.* Seminar Series 204. Melbourne: Center for Strategic Education.

Fullan, M. (2013). *Stratosphere: Integrating technology, pedagogy, and change knowledge.* Toronto: Pearson.

Fullan, M. (2014). *The principal: Three keys for maximizing impact.* San Francisco: Jossey-Bass.

Fullan, M., & Quinn, J. (2015). *Coherence: The right drivers in action.* Thousand Oaks, CA: Corwin Press.

Fullan, M., & Rincon-Gallardo, S. (in press). Developing high-quality public education in Canada: The case of Ontario. In F. Adamson & L. Darling-Hammond (Eds.), *Global education reform: Privatization vs public investments in national education systems.* London: Routledge Press.

Fullan, M., Rincon-Gallardo, S., & Hargreaves, A. (2015). Professional capital as accountability. *Education Policy*

Analysis Archives, 23(15). http://dx.doi.org/10.14507/epaa .v23.1998.

Gallup. (2014). *The state of the American workplace.* Washington, DC: Author.

Hargreaves, A., Boyle, A., & Harris, A. (2014). *Uplifting leadership: How organizations, teams, and communities raise performance.* San Francisco, CA: Jossey-Bass.

Hargreaves, A., & Braun, H. (2012). *Leading for all: A research report of the development, design, implementation and impact of Ontario's "Essential for Some, Good for All" initiative.* Boston, MA: Boston College.

Hargreaves, A., & Fullan, M. (2012). *Professional capital: Transforming teaching in every school.* New York, NY: Teachers College Press.

Hargreaves, A., & Shirley, D. (2012). *The global fourth way.* Thousand Oaks, CA: Corwin Press.

Hattie, J. (2009). *Visible learning: A synthesis of over 800 meta-analyses relating to achievement.* London and New York, NY: Routledge.

Holiday, R. (2014). *The obstacle is the way.* New York, NY: Penguin Books.

Huffington, A. (2014). *Thrive: The third metric to redefining success and creating a life of well-being, wisdom, and wonder.* New York, NY: Harmony Books.

Hung, D. (2014). A system's model of scaling: Centralization and decentralization balances. Singapore: Ministry of Education.

Irving, J. (1982). *Groupthink: Psychological studies of policy decisions and fiascoes.* Boston, MA: Houghton-Mifflin.

Isaacson, W. (2014). *The innovators: How a group of hackers, geniuses, and geeks created the digital revolution.* New York, NY: Simon & Schuster.

Johnson, S. M. (2004). *Finders and keepers: Helping new teachers thrive and survive in our schools.* San Francisco, CA: Jossey-Bass.

Khosla, S., & Sawhney, M. (2014). *Fewer, bigger, bolder.* New York, NY: Penguin Group.

Kluger, J. (2008). *Simplexity.* New York, NY: Hyperion.

Leanna, C. (2011). The missing link in school reform. *Stanford Social Innovation Review, 9*(4), 30–35.

Lencioni, P. (2007). *The three signs of a miserable job.* San Francisco, CA: Jossey-Bass.

Livingston, A. (1935, May 25). Vilfredo Pareto: A biographical portrait. *Saturday Review,* p. 12.

LRN. (2014). *The freedom report.* New York, NY: Author.

Mehta, J. (2013). *The allure of order: High hopes, dashed expectations, and the troubled quest to remake American schooling.* New York, NY: Oxford University Press.

Metropolitan Life Insurance. (2013). *The MetLife survey of the American teacher.* New York, NY: Author.

Mintzberg, H. (2015). *Rebalancing society: Radical renewal beyond left, right, and center.* Oakland, CA: Berrett-Koehler Publishers.

Morieux, Y., & Tollman, P. (2014). *Six simple rules: How to manage complexity without getting complicated.* Boston, MA: Harvard University Review Press.

Niver, L. (2013, November 5). Why so many of America's teachers are leaving the profession. *Post 50 (Huffington Post* blog). Retrieved from http://www.huffingtonpost.com /lisa-niver-rajna/teaching-profession_b_4172238.html

Organization for Economic Cooperation and Development. (2014a). *PISA 2013 results.* Paris: Author.

Organization for Economic Cooperation and Development. (2014b). *TALIS 2013: An international perspective on teaching and learning.* Paris: Author.

Pareto, V. (1935). *The mind and society* (4 vols.). A. Livingston (Ed.). New York, NY: Harcourt Brace.

Pentland, A. (2014). *Social physics: How good ideas spread— the lessons from a new science.* New York, NY: Penguin Press.

Pink, D. (2009). *Drive: The surprising truth about what motivates us.* New York, NY: Riverhead Books.

Rincon-Gallardo, S., & Fullan, M. (2015). The social physics of educational change: Essential features of effective collaboration. Unpublished paper: www.michaelfullan.ca.

Rogers, E. (2003). *Diffusion of innovations* (5th ed.). New York, NY: Free Press.

Rosenberg, T. (2011). *Join the club: How peer pressure can transform the world.* New York, NY: Norton.

Rothfeder, J. (2014). *Driving Honda: Inside the world's most innovative car company.* New York, NY: Penguin Group.

Sisodia, R., Wolfe, D., & Sheth, J. (2007). *Firms of endearment: How world-class companies profit from passion and purpose.* Upper Saddle River, NJ: Wharton School Publishing.

Stone, D., & Heen, S. (2014). *Thanks for the feedback.* New York, NY: Viking.

Storr, A. (1989). *Solitude.* London: Fontana Paperbacks.

Sutton, R., & Rao, H. (2014). *Scaling up excellence: Getting to more without settling for less.* New York, NY: Crown Business.

TINYpulse. (2014). *The 7 key trends impacting today's workplace.* Retrieved from http://www.tinyhr.com/2014-employee-engagement-organizational-culture-report

INDEX